Praise for *Easier Than You Think*

There is no one I trust more in the real estate investor circle than Mike Hanna. No one has more integrity, and his experience is second to none. In *Easier Than You Think*, Mike lays out the most straightforward approach to single-family real estate investing that will benefit anyone getting started. Put it at the top of your reading list!

  —Joe Pollard, CEO, Vedero Software

I've been investing in real estate for over 10 years, and I can honestly say that Mike's book has totally nailed it! This book spells out the process, in easy to understand language, exactly how anyone can leverage real estate to help build true wealth and invite abundance into their lives.

  —Steve Skains, Investor and National Trainer

Success often comes down to surrounding yourself with the right people, and getting information from those that have learned lessons the hard way (on your behalf). Mike Hanna is "the right people", and his straightforward book shares his lessons learned to help you get started. Real Estate Investing really is a pretty simple business—but you can make it as complicated as you'd like. Do yourself a favor—read this book, and commit to keeping it simple.

  —Mike Hambright, Chief Nerd, FlipNerd.com

Easier Than You Think is a real world approach to real estate investing that will definitely help anyone who wants to succeed. If you want to take your investing to the next level, I highly encourage you to read this book.

  —Chasen Smith, Owner, Prime Holdings

Mike Hanna is genuinely interested in helping new real estate investors succeed. He knows the business start to finish, and has been a valued mentor and friend for many years.

  —Jerry Davidson, Real Estate Investor and Client

This book is clearly written and provides anyone interested in understanding the details of building a real-estate investment business, an invaluable resource. Mike writes with a style that is easy to read but doesn't skimp on the details that may intimidate someone wanting to get started. I would recommend it to anyone as a must read!

 —Andreas Melder, Serial Entrepreneur

This book offers many insights into the practical aspects of real estate investing. The answers to many questions beginning investors have are thoroughly discussed, along with many relevant examples. I highly recommend it to anyone looking for a reliable guide to real estate investment success.

 —Tiep Truong, MD

Mike's shows his years of experience by simplifying the complex world of real estate investing. He answers the questions you didn't know you had, and definitely puts the reader on a path to success.

 —Maureen McGuire, President, Texas Republic Bank

Easier Than You Think

AN EXPERT'S GUIDE TO SINGLE FAMILY REAL ESTATE INVESTING

Mike Hanna

Circumference Press

Easier Than You Think: An Expert's Guide to Single Family Real Estate Investing

Cover art by Shannon Durst

Interior layout by Jonathan Peters, PhD

ISBN: 978-0-9903262-6-7

Printed in the United States of America

CONTENTS

This book is dedicated to my amazing wife Mary Jane, and my loving daughters Audrey and Rachel.

*P*ROLOGUE

In some ways you could say September 2003 was a turning point for me.

My wife and I had just moved into a new house with our three-year-old daughter, I got fired from my job, and then my wife told me she was pregnant with our second daughter. And that was all in the first week! What's more, we were unable to sell our previous home, and instead, it became a rental. So there was a lot of stress at that time and pressure to make things work.

Looking to make a career change, I decided to go into real estate full time. I didn't even know what that meant, but I had a family to take care of and was determined to figure it out quickly. I already owned some rental properties with a couple of partners and decided to start there by working with them to expand our portfolio within the partnership.

Burning Through Savings

Since the properties didn't provide enough cash flow to support taking a salary, I liquidated my 401(k), moved my investment portfolio to cash, and throughout the next year purchased more rentals with my partners, all while burning through more of my savings. If you've been there, I know you understand how expensive a four-year-old and six-month-old can get in addition to all of life's other expenses. If you haven't, trust me, it can be significant. Looking at my dwindling bank account, it didn't take long to figure out something had to change before I'd burned through all of my reserves.

To add to the level of stress I was experiencing, I would get random calls from recruiters checking in with me to see if I was interested in interviewing for a software sales job, my prior profession. Since my financial situation was eroding, this was very tempting to consider. This created a mental battle about what was the right thing to do for my family. *Do I move forward with real estate investing or get a full time job?*

I actually went on an interview just to investigate one of the opportunities presented to me. It required full-time travel away from my family to work for some technology company that didn't seem to know where it was going. Needless to say, I became disinterested about ten minutes into the interview. I stayed for the rest of the painful interview as a courtesy, when I should have politely told them this was not for me and just left. The entire time all I could think about were the real estate calls I needed to take and the appointments I had for later that day. I knew I would never be happy returning to that world, and this interview cemented this decision for me.

I ultimately turned down every recruiter call and told them to take me off their list.

Changing Direction

To raise some money and move in a different direction, I sold both my interest in the partnership and my former home to the tenants that were living there. Having made a decent profit on both, I put all of that money into real estate and began wholesaling properties. This wasn't easy. In fact, wholesaling took time to figure out. At that time, the Dallas/Fort Worth real estate investor market was not nearly as diverse as it is today.

Back then, for a wholesale deal to sell, it had to be priced much lower than today's market pricing, or selling it could be a nightmare. It took about nine months before I started getting some consistent and somewhat predictable income.

The First House I Tried to Flip

I was improving as a wholesaler but really wanted to make a larger profit. I found my first deal to flip and was in a competitive situation with another investor/buyer. I decided to pay a bit more for the deal in order to secure it, because I believed I was going to make at least $20,000 after all expenses. I was totally wrong.

MY INITIAL ESTIMATES

AFTER REPAIR VALUE

$105,000

MINUS (-)

PURCHASE PRICE: (-) $55,000
SCOPE OF WORK: (-) $20,000
OTHER COSTS: (-) $10,000

NET PROFIT: $20,000

ACTUAL NUMBERS

AFTER REPAIR VALUE

$96,000

MINUS (-)

PURCHASE PRICE: (-) $55,000
SCOPE OF WORK: (-) $30,000
OTHER COSTS: (-) $11,000

NET PROFIT: $0

I purchased the house for $55,000, and like most beginners, I overestimated the value, underestimated the repairs, and basically paid too much for the house. In *Chapter 8: Flipping Property*, I will discuss each one of these components and how not to make these mistakes.

So, what was supposed to be a flip was now going to be a rental. However, I got it rented and refinanced where it produced $430 per month in positive cash flow. Each month, I collect rent, make mortgage payments, and increase my equity through principal reduction.

With enough patience, this turned out to be a great deal that I am happy owning. I still own this property as of this writing, and the value has increased to $140,000. The rent has also increased $200 per month improving my cash flow to $630. Having sold my interest in several rental properties I owned in a partnership, I wanted to get back into this side of the business. Over the next several years, I was able to accomplish this by acquiring both single-family and multi-family properties. I also flipped several houses and made a profit on each one.

Lessons Learned

Making this first mistake showed me that real estate investing was nothing like the stock market. Your stock in a company can go to zero. I know because I had some that came close to zero. Let me tell you, it's a horrible feeling. A rent house you own, however, is not going to zero. Even if it goes down in value, you can still have cash flow. Real estate investing is not as sexy as the stock market, but it's also not as risky in my opinion. Done correctly, real estate investing can be very exciting and produce enormous returns over time.

*I*NTRODUCTION

I had many people read this book before it went to press so I could get some feedback, and of course, some endorsements. The feedback I received was exactly what I had hoped to convey in the text. Things like "for serious investors only," "quality content," "detailed," and "blueprint for success," just to name some. I am flattered by those comments and glad to hear the value is there from the reader's perspective.

Real estate investing can be overwhelming, especially when you are brand new in the business. There's so much noise in the real estate investing world that many new investors don't know where to begin or how to get started. Just walk down the isle of any major bookstore or get on Amazon and search for real estate investing books. There are tons of books on flipping houses, wholesaling property, and rental property investing, along with books on creative techniques that get many investors into trouble. How does anyone know what resources they need? Trying to consume all of this information just to figure out what to do and how to do it is a huge burden, and prevents many investors from getting started.

There are entire books written on topics I cover as chapters in this text. I don't know about you, but I bet you don't want to read multiple books on flipping houses, or multiple books on a single investing strategy and get bogged down with so many details, that you decide to give up before you get started. My guess is if you are reading this book, you probably want a resource that can cover all of this at one time. If that's true, you came to the right place.

Most of what you will learn in real estate is by doing it. It's not any more complicated than that. You learn to play an instrument by playing the instrument. You learn to drive a car by getting behind the wheel and putting the car in gear. The same is true for real estate investing. But to get you started, you need a guide that can be a reference for you for any investing strategy you take.

This book covers the keys to getting started, the top three investing strategies, performing due diligence correctly, finding deals, successfully making offers, as well as one of the most powerful things you can do right now to take your investing career to the next level. I wrote this book to condense what I believe is the most important information you will need to make success in real estate investing **Easier Than You Think**. I hope you enjoy it, and I hope that it helps you achieve your real estate goals, no matter what they happen to be.

SECTION ONE
LAYING THE FOUNDATION FOR REAL ESTATE INVESTING

Easier Than You Think

CHAPTER 1

WHAT YOU'RE GOING TO GET FROM THIS BOOK

You probably already know that real estate investing is the most powerful tool for building passive income and long-term wealth. You may have heard a speaker talk about this at a local investor club, heard some guru on the radio, or read a book (or several books) on the topic of real estate investing. Or, you may know someone who is an investor and have witnessed their success.

Can you think of another investment vehicle that pays you five different ways like rental properties do? The answer? There isn't one. If there were, I would absolutely be doing it.

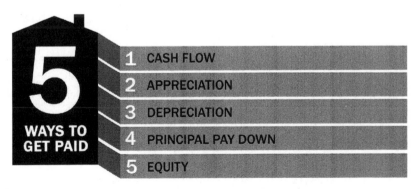

5 WAYS TO GET PAID

1. CASH FLOW
2. APPRECIATION
3. DEPRECIATION
4. PRINCIPAL PAY DOWN
5. EQUITY

Real estate is also a powerful tool for providing immediate income through wholesaling, as well as for turning a quick profit by making tangible improvements and flipping the property. So there are multiple ways to invest in real estate and make money.

THE LAYOUT AND PURPOSE OF THIS BOOK

The purpose of this book is to provide you with the tools you need to get started and have success going forward. Some of the things I discuss here I learned from books. Some were learned from others' experiences. But most of what I'll share with you I learned by actually doing real estate deals, making mistakes, and studying better ways to succeed.

What I have included in this book is what I believe every real estate investor needs to understand to successfully get started, whether wholesaling, flipping, building passive income through rental properties, or creating long-term wealth by holding property and building equity. Even if you have no experience doing any of these things, I have no doubt that you can have success with any one of them. You just have to stay focused, use the information here, and take it one step at a time.

WHAT MAKES THIS BOOK SO SPECIAL?

Fair question! Aren't there enough books out there on real estate investing? Sure there are. I have read many of them. Did I get anything out of those books? Yes, I did. But many left me hanging on the "how to" or were more motivational and inspiring than filled with the kind of hands-on knowledge I needed to take action.

After reading some of these books, I started to wonder if the author was actually in the real estate investing business or just someone trying to sell books. It always bothers me when some so-called guru makes more money from teaching a topic than they make actually doing it. This book was written by someone who actually is a successful real estate investor.

Also, some books out there have ideas that are outdated or contain concepts that are now illegal to do. The laws are changing. With the signing of Dodd Frank in 2010 (an extremely large bill passed by Congress), as well as laws passed by some states, limitations have been placed on things that were commonplace a few years ago. With the 2016 election results, even more changes could be on the way.

Speaking of the law, let's talk about attorneys and legal advice for a moment.

USING ATTORNEYS AND GETTING LEGAL ADVICE

One thing many new and experienced investors face is the need to get legal advice. All too often new investors try to find this information online, or get it from friends who are not legal professionals. This is a huge mistake because most real estate laws are governed by your state and there are of course, federal laws as well. There is so much disinformation online that it's downright scary. There are also so called "gurus" teaching things in different states that are actually illegal in that state!

If you are new to this business and have never been in business for yourself, you are probably like most people and scared of lawyers and think they are too expensive. Get over it. At some point you are going to need to use an attorney.

Attorneys are an important tool in your shed, so don't discount them. Think of them as a critical asset and part of your team. In most cases, they are not too expensive if you are using a specialist (i.e. a real estate legal expert), and you have your questions prepared ahead of a meeting. You are looking for someone who isn't going to bill you for a lot of research because they already know the answer.

You will be more successful using the right attorney and will be confident in what you are doing, instead of taking a chance on doing something the wrong way or worse, illegal! If for nothing else, just getting some advice about what to do in a given situation can be invaluable.

In fact, you are probably going to need more than one attorney. I can hear some of you saying, "Oh no! I thought I would never have to use one, and now you are saying I may need another?" Oh yes, you will. I currently use several attorneys, and in the beginning of my real estate investing career, I never thought I would need more than one.

The reason I use many attorneys: *business is not complicated, but the law certainly can be.* I have one attorney who is a real estate expert with over 45 years of experience. He is my go-to person when I need the answer now. Most of the time he knows it right away, has had cases exactly like it, and doesn't need to spend any time looking up the answer (which saves me money). He also doesn't go to court as part of his legal practice. Therefore, I need someone else who can handle small court related issues.

I also have an attorney who sets up entities for me and files all the appropriate documents with the state. He happens to be a really good corporate attorney who also understands real estate. Can I set these entities up myself? Yes, but I don't want to spend the time doing this, and it's a relatively small flat fee that I pay, and it gives me peace of mind that everything was done correctly.

It takes time to find the right attorney, and my suggestion is to ask around in your real estate investor community to find one that you are comfortable using. Find full time real estate investors who have been in the business a long time (over five years) and have done multiple deals. They will know an attorney(s) you can use. Or better yet, find an investor who has been in the business for 15+ years or more. They will certainly have more than one that they have used and can reference.

This book is not going to cover anything overly *creative* that looks for some loophole in the law or does anything illegal. You can be wildly successful without doing anything like this, and I will show you how. If you are looking to learn how to skate around the laws and do things on the edge of what's legal, *this book is not for you.*

This book is, however, filled with the best content available in today's market, based on personal experience doing several hundred deals, as well as being the lender for my investor clients in over 1,000 loans. However, no matter what any book says (including this one), there is no substitute for actual experience. Your experience may differ from mine, since no two deals are alike.

Easier Than You Think

CHAPTER 2

WHAT IS A REAL ESTATE INVESTOR?

Before we discuss anything else, let's talk about what a real investor is. Most of this book will focus on specific strategies and due diligence, ultimately leading to working actual real estate deals. But to do that, we need to make sure we're all on the same page. There's a lot of confusing (and even bad) information out there, and you might have the wrong idea about what being a real estate investor means.

WHAT A REAL ESTATE INVESTOR IS NOT

I recently watched a documentary about the 2008 market crash. In one of the segments, they interviewed homeowners who borrowed against the equity in their home, anticipating the value would go up so they could sell the house and make a profit. I'm sure you have heard stories like this and may even know people who did this.

In the documentary, these people were viewed as "real estate investors" who were speculating and ended up getting burned because the value of their home actually went down and they were underwater (owed more than the house was worth). Anyone not in the real estate business might believe these people are real estate investors, but this isn't what those of us in the industry mean when we use the term.

For better or worse, this is how real estate investors are most often portrayed in the media. This, of course, is totally absurd. A homeowner is *NOT* a real estate investor. Your home, contrary to what you have heard, is not your biggest asset. In most cases, it's your biggest *liability*. It pays you nothing, and in fact, can become a bottomless pit of money.

Now don't think I have something against home ownership. I love home ownership. I just don't think someone is a real estate investor simply because they purchased a homestead.

Also, "speculating" is not in the vocabulary of any successful real estate investor. By speculating, I mean buying a property with the expectation or hope that it will be able to be sold for a profit, usually due to positive market conditions, but doing so with the risk of a loss.

Furthermore, a real estate investor is not a handyman, painter, plumber, electrician, landscaper, etc. It doesn't matter if you are one of these by trade or not; you should not be at your investment house fixing it up, making improvements to it yourself, or doing any type of work to it personally. Separate your day job from your investments.

What should you be doing? Focus on managing tradesmen and finding your next deal.

So, What Is a Real Estate Investor?

Are you a real estate investor if you just flip houses? Is it only considered *investing* if you buy and hold rental property? What if you just wholesale deals? Is that considered investing? Without getting into semantics, if you buy (or contract to buy) real estate for purposes of making a profit (i.e., not planning to live there), you are a real estate investor.

REAL ESTATE INVESTORS: GREEDY PROFITEERS OR GOOD SAMARITANS?

Now that we understand what a real estate investor is, I want to cover something else. I am proud to be a real estate investor, but in the many years I have been in this business, I have heard the most inaccurate, absurd, as well as offensive things about real estate investors. Things like, we are greedy profiteers or slumlords. Probably the most outrageous was told to one of my real estate friends by his banker, "We are in an evil business." Imagine that. Who would say something like this, except someone who doesn't truly understand what we do as real estate investors?

The Often Overlooked True Value of Real Estate Investing

I want to set the record straight, so when you hear things like this you can respond with the facts and be proud to call yourself a real estate investor.

Real estate investors add more value to a distressed community than anyone else. This may sound bold, but it's absolutely true. Whether you wholesale, flip, or own rental properties, you are adding tremendous value to the community by taking risks others won't. And guess what? You should make money doing it! If there were no incentive, and no one willing to put their time and money at risk, entire communities would deteriorate.

When you drive through a neighborhood and see that awful house, you know the one I am talking about, the one with three-foot-tall weeds, 15 newspapers in the yard, mail covering the front porch, broken windows with stray animals going in and out, etc., you see opportunity. The neighbors see a bad situation that won't go away fast enough because, from their perspective, no one cares enough to do anything.

Even worse is when the city takes action and boards up the house, creating a false impression that this is a bad neighborhood. Think about this for a minute. If you saw two houses like this on the same street, what would you think? How about three on the same street?

17

When this happens, the value of the neighborhood can completely erode along with the property tax revenue, in turn affecting schools, hospitals, and even essential services like police and fire. There is less desirability for a homebuyer to purchase a home in a neighborhood with three boarded up houses on the street. Safety becomes the number one concern in these situations, and fear will make buyers look elsewhere.

I once had a tenant from Detroit who retired to Dallas. I remember asking him what it was like living in Detroit. He said he was scared all the time. He lived in the inner city, and most of the houses on his street were vacant. Moving for him was a blessing because he escaped the cold weather as well as a dangerous neighborhood. This happened because no investors were willing to take on the risk where he lived.

When a real estate investor finally steps in to improve a property, the value of the neighboring property increases, the tax assessed value increases, the neighborhood feels safer and more desirable, and families want to live there. For you to take on this level of responsibility, you need to be rewarded financially, and you need to feel great about what you are doing.

So when you hear anything negative about real estate investors, remember to counter back with what I mentioned, in a way that is confident, courteous, and professional, because no one is doing more for distressed communities than real estate investors.

CHAPTER 3

THE KEYS TO GETTING STARTED

One of the hardest things to do in life is get started. Whether it's a new job, a new business, or a new relationship. All of these involve challenges because of the unknown, the unforeseen, and a general lack of knowledge and experience. This can create anxiety and fear, which can prevent you from taking the next steps to move forward on a path to success. The same is also true for getting started in real estate investing.

I want to help anyone struggling with this to get past it so they can really understand what it takes to get started in real estate investing. I have outlined what I believe are four keys for putting you on a path to success. So let's dive in:

KEY #1: KNOW YOUR REAL ESTATE INVESTING STRATEGIES

What I would like for you to do at this point is to get a feel for the three strategies we are going to discuss in the upcoming chapters. We are going to get into greater detail about these, but for now, I want you to start thinking about them so they can be top of mind. They are wholesaling property, flipping property, and owning rental property.

1. **Wholesaling Property**: This, for the most part, is a transaction-oriented business. Think of it as flipping a contract to purchase a property. The concept is simple, and can be done in different ways:

   (1) Find a property that you can buy at a discount

   (2) Get it under contract with the seller

   (3) Sell that contract to another buyer for a fee

   How much can you make on a given transaction? Fair question. I have personally seen wholesale deals with my hard-money clients where a contract was sold for over $50,000 (this of course is rare, but totally possible), and some for $500 or less. It depends on:

   (1) How good your purchase price is

   (2) How much your end buyer is willing to pay

   One of the biggest benefits to wholesaling is ease of entry into the business. You can also do it with very little money out of pocket. As long as you find the right deal, you can move it to someone who will pay more.

2. **Flipping Property**: This, in my opinion, is the profit-oriented approach to real estate investing. The concept is this:

   (1) Buy property at a discount to market value

   (2) Make the necessary tangible improvements

   (3) Sell it at retail price

   I have flipped a lot of properties, and so have many of my clients. Flipping property tends to get a bad rap in the media primarily because it is misunderstood, but it is without a doubt a great way to turn a quick profit (larger than with wholesaling), and also helps improve many neighborhoods and communities.

3. **Rental Property**: This is the passive income/ long-term wealth building approach to real estate investing. Rental properties, if purchased correctly,

should produce positive monthly cash flow, while simultaneously increasing your equity through principal reduction. This means your tenants' rent payment will provide you with monthly income after you make your mortgage payment. Each mortgage payment you make has an interest portion and a principal portion, so each month, as principal is paid, your equity in the property increases.

KEY #2: GET A SPECIFIC GOAL DOWN ON PAPER

The biggest key to getting started is setting a goal and writing it down on paper. I know I'm preaching to the choir with some, though others might be thinking, "You've got to be kidding me! Is this going to be another book about goal setting?"

Even if you think this is cliché, follow me for a minute here; how are you ever going to get where you want to be with your real estate investing if you don't have some idea or goal in mind? How will you be able to measure if you are getting there? Do you really want to leave it up to chance? Wouldn't it be better to take charge and have a plan?

If you want to go to the movies, do you just hop in the car, start driving, and hope you end up at a place with the movie you want to see showing within 30 minutes of your arrival? *Of course not*! How much more important is it then, to have a goal for the really important things in your life—like building real income and wealth? So you need a goal to plan your path and measure your progress. For your goal to be measurable, it needs to be *specific*. Here are some examples of goals:

EXAMPLE GOALS

1. BUY ONE RENTAL HOUSE THIS YEAR TO INCREASE YOUR POSITIVE CASH FLOW EACH MONTH BY $400.
2. FLIP TWO HOUSES THIS YEAR FOR A COMBINED NET PROFIT OF $40,000.
3. WHOLESALE THREE HOUSES THIS YEAR FOR A COMBINED NET INCOME OF $25,000.

These are just examples. Use them, tweak them, or don't (although they are likely good starter goals for most readers). If you have your own goal, great! One thing I want to mention about this is thinking in terms of not what is "realistic," but what is "attainable" for you. If you set your goal to something that is not attainable, you are likely going to be disappointed, get frustrated, and quit.

The best advice I can give you if you don't know what goal to set is to start with a single deal. Use that to build some valuable experience, and then move on to the next deal. I promise that you'll learn so much from that first deal, that before you know it, you'll be well on your way. Plus, you'll have gained some momentum, which will only build the further along you get.

KEY #3: NETWORK WITH OTHER REAL ESTATE INVESTORS

Other real estate investors are going to be your best resource for networking, creating your mastermind group, and building the rest of your team. You want to reach out to them, learn from them, and discuss your ideas with them first.

If you decide after reading this book (or worse, while you are reading it) to start telling everyone you know that you are going to start investing in real estate, my advice is DON'T do it, especially if they have never invested in real estate. Why? Here are a couple of reasons:

1. **Some people will try to talk you out of it.** No one is better at talking you out of taking action than the guy next to you who literally knows nothing about real estate investing. He will bring you down faster than a lead balloon. There is nothing worse than getting "advice" from someone who knows absolutely nothing about a subject. It's funny that people who know nothing about a topic love to tell people what they think about it. Consider this, if your tooth hurts and you are in massive pain, would you discuss it with the plumber fixing your toilet? Of

course not. What does he know about fixing tooth-aches? Nothing! Guess what? Your coworker doesn't know anything about real estate investing, so don't tell him/her what your plans are.

2. **The more you talk about something, the less likely you will actually do it.** There is a great quote by Walt Disney who said, "The way to get started is to quit talking and start doing." This is a fact that people talk about something (like a great idea) and never do it because they have talked it to death, and the interest, excitement, and any passion that was there has evaporated with every word out of their mouth. Consider this, how many times have you thought about a great idea and didn't stop talking about it? How long was it before you totally lost interest in it?

KEY #4: TAKE ACTION!

To recap, the first three keys are:

1. Understanding your investing strategies
2. Having a goal written down on paper
3. Keeping your plans to yourself

After this, you must take action by utilizing the knowledge you gain from this book to evaluate deals and move on them. There are lots of resources out there on the topic of taking action for those who struggle with it. You may be highly motivated, and will have no trouble getting started after reading this book. Or you might have a difficult time getting out of your comfort zone. If so, I want to help you take action right now. Go find a pen and paper and write down your action plan. Seriously, I want you to do this.

If you are struggling this, I have included a sample action plan in the graphic on the following page. Also, you can go to YouTube and watch "How to Take Action" by Tony Robbins. That will help put things in perspective for you.

ACTION PLAN

1 I WILL FINISH READING THIS BOOK SO THAT I UNDERSTAND MY INVESTING STRATEGIES AND HOW TO IMPLEMENT THEM.

2 I WILL WRITE DOWN MY REAL ESTATE INVESTING GOAL(S) FOR THIS YEAR AND KEEP IT WITH ME.

3 I WILL NOT TELL ANYONE WHO IS NOT A REAL ESTATE INVESTOR WHAT MY PLAN OR GOAL IS.

CHAPTER 4

THE POWER OF A MASTERMIND GROUP

You have probably heard the saying, "No man is an island" by John Donne, a 17th Century English author. One of the members of my mastermind group said this at the first meeting we attended as the reason he wanted to be part of it. It has resonated with me to this day. Translation: No one person is 100% self-sufficient. We all rely on others at different points in our lives. Not only in our personal lives but also in business. I believe having a team that you can depend on in a business environment is critical to your success.

Now this might not be evident if you've never been in a mastermind group before, but I want to make it absolutely clear that one of the most valuable assets you can possibly have for taking your real estate investing (or any business endeavor) to the next level, is a mastermind group. I can tell you in all honesty that I would not have the portfolio, the resources, or the knowledge base I have today without my mastermind group. In fact, most of what I know about real estate investing came from being part of my mastermind group.

I learned how to buy deals correctly, protest property taxes, find the best real estate attorneys, create special provisions to my leases, find my property manager, find my CPA, as well as excellent tradesman for any type of work—all from my master-mind group. I've learned more than I can possibly relate here, but literally, I've found resources on anything involved with real estate investing from difficult situations with tenants and clients, code enforcement, the city, contractors, etc., from my group. I have also done multiple deals with everyone in my group—we all do business with one another.

I cannot stress enough how profound of an impact it will have on your real estate investing. So if you are currently not in a mastermind group, I encourage you to get one started ASAP.

SO WHAT IS A MASTERMIND GROUP ANYWAY?

The concept of a mastermind group comes from Napoleon Hill's book, *Think and Grow Rich*. If you haven't read it, I highly encourage you do so. At least read the chapter on the mastermind concept. For now, you can watch YouTube videos where Napoleon explains the concept if it's completely brand new to you.

Hill defines a mastermind as, "Coordination of knowledge and effort, in a spirit of harmony, between two or more people, for the attainment of a definite purpose." Basically, the concept is *the whole is greater than the sum of the parts.* Or, 1 + 1 = 3. The point is that two brains together are actually equivalent to three brains on their own. This principal works exponentially the more minds you add. So imagine the power of 15 people. This synergy will produce valuable information that will take your real estate investing to the next level.

WHO DO YOU NEED IN A MASTERMIND GROUP?

There is no hard and fast rule about who must be in your group. For example, our group consists of full-time real estate investors, and everyone owns rental property. We have agents, brokers, an appraiser, some lenders, an accountant, a financial planner, and some wholesalers as members. However, we weren't looking for those types of backgrounds when we got started; it just happened to evolve with those individuals. Just to give you an idea of the volume of business we do, combined we close over 100 transactions each month.

What's key is that those in your mastermind group are open, honest, and trust each other. We have no secrets, and no one would ever go behind anyone's back in a deal—*this is exactly what you want*. We discuss everything openly, and I consider everyone core members of my real estate investing team.

STARTING YOUR OWN MASTERMIND GROUP

So how do you start a mastermind group for yourself? You begin by networking with people in the real estate investor community (i.e., local investor clubs, meetup groups, etc.) Find those people who are at your level or higher—those who have different backgrounds but share your goal of getting to the next level in their real estate investing career. This is *VITAL*.

Focus on finding someone with similar interests, whether that be building a rental portfolio, flipping houses, etc., and start meeting with them on a regular basis. Then, add a third person that you both agree to bring into your group. Have a meeting or two with them and then find another person and add them. Don't rush into adding too many people at one time or feel like you have to build a large group immediately. This is about quality, not quantity. You need to build strong relationships of trust.

SETTING THE GROUND RULES FOR YOUR MASTERMIND GROUP

As with any organization, it's important to have a set of rules or guidelines that everyone can follow, so that meetings will be taken seriously, and you will make the most productive use of time. After a few meetings, it will become easier to get a feel for how you want to structure them. You certainly don't have to do it the way I am going to describe, but after ten years of meetings, I have found the following to be most effective:

- **Group Size**: We have a group of 15 members. We found that 15 people is about as many as we can have and still get through the meeting in a productive manner.

- **Frequency**: Currently, we meet every other week on the same day for two hours, unless it's a holiday. Initially we met once a week, but this was too much for most members. You can do once a week if you think that works, it likely will when you are getting started. The key is finding something that works for your group the way we did. Don't be afraid to fine tune the frequency of your meetings.

- **Agenda**: Our agenda is simple (and of course yours can vary): 9:00 AM to 9:15 arrive and order breakfast, 9:15 to 11:00 roundtable discussion. During the roundtable, each person has about five to seven minutes to discuss what they are working on and/or bring up any issues they are seeing or experiencing in the market. We also have a "Did you know...?" option where members can share information they heard or read somewhere that would benefit the group. Remember, this is not a social hour or networking event. When you bring everyone together in this environment there can be a tendency to socialize, get off topic, and waste a lot of time. If you are leading the group, be sure to keep everyone focused and on track.

- **Participation is Key**: You want a group where everyone participates in the roundtable discussions. If you have this, meetings take on a life of their own. This is where the real "mastermind" takes place. Once everyone has heard from the rest of the group, the meeting can take on a new form where members can jump into the conversation and share what they believe would add value and benefit the entire group.

- **Attendance Policy**: It's important to have commitment from everyone to attend every meeting (or most meetings). You are probably going to have some people in your group who will show up once, commit, and then never attend. Others will come to half of the meetings. It's your call what to do here, but to get the most benefit, you need to have attendance commitment. For people who commit and never attend, I suggest you remove them from the group.

- **Adding New Members**: Once your group is going with a small amount of hand-selected members, you may want to consider some additions. The best way to invite a new member is have them come as a guest who everyone agrees would bring value. Don't mention joining, just ask them to attend. During the meeting, it will become obvious if they would add value to the group. However, it's best to get everyone's feedback on that person after the meeting, perhaps through a phone call or email. If there is opposition, consider NOT bringing them on board. Don't create animosity or resentment between members. Be certain to not tell that person they can attend again before checking with everyone to prevent an awkward situation.

- **Removing Members**: It's important to have the right people in your group to have the most success. You may have to remove more than one person, so don't be afraid to do this. Anyone who never shows up, is toxic in the group, is a pessimist, or brings the meetings down, needs to be removed. If you don't, you will regret it because other members will leave your group. Removing someone from the group can be easy or very difficult, depending on the person. If it's someone who doesn't show up, you can send an email to everyone in the group that goes something like the following:

  We have had some members who have not attended many of the meetings. I am requesting that anyone who does not want to participate, to please let me know, and we can remove you from the email invitation.

If it's someone who is negative or toxic to the meetings, it's more than likely someone who adds no value and is not doing anything in this business. If that's the case, I would personally call them and explain the fact that based on feedback from the group, they may not be the right fit, and you are going to remove them from the email invitation list.

Conclusion

Find the right people and the right venue, and you will enjoy every meeting. After your first meeting, you will experience the value I have described here, and will soon watch your real estate investing accelerate to the next level.

SECTION TWO:
INVESTING
STRATEGIES

CHAPTER 5

YOUR REAL ESTATE INVESTING STRATEGIES

Welcome to Section Two! Before we get into making great deals, we need to understand the investing strategies available to you that I briefly mentioned at the beginning of the book. We need to dive into this in more detail so you don't pass on a deal just because it doesn't meet your objectives.

For example, if your objective is making a large profit, you are probably going to be focused on flipping property. If you find a deal where the equity spread is not big enough for you to comfortably make the profit you desire, *DON'T walk away from the deal!* Instead, remember your other two strategies. Depending on the numbers, it could make a great rental property for someone, or someone else may be comfortable with a lower profit margin than you.

INVESTING STRATEGIES: A QUICK RECAP

How do you determine if the house you are evaluating meets the criteria of being a "deal?" This is a great question. The reality is that it's subjective and ultimately depends on what you are trying to accomplish. Many times, a potential deal lends itself to one strategy over another. Here are some questions to ask yourself if you need help determining which strategy is best for you:

1. Do you want immediate income? Then wholesaling is for you.

2. Are you looking to make a large profit? You need to focus on flipping property.

3. Are you seeking passive income and looking to create long-term wealth? Start building a rental portfolio.

Maybe you want to do all of these things or a combination? There is absolutely nothing wrong with that. In fact, that is the best approach in my opinion because you will turn down fewer deals and be able to do something with each one that comes your way.

As much as I don't want to tell anyone what to do, I must state this: *You need to be able to do all three of these.* Each of these goes hand in hand with one another. If you are not comfortable with one or more of these strategies, the upcoming sections are going to help by giving you the knowledge to succeed in each of them. However, you may not always be in a position to do all three because some require more money than others. We'll discuss this when we discuss financing deals later on. So the goal is to never have to worry about money being the issue.

Throughout the rest of this section, we'll explore in detail the three primary investing strategies that you can utilize to find your deals: wholesaling, flipping and rentals.

SECTION TWO GLOSSARY

At the start of each section, I will go over the significant terms we'll encounter. You can find a full list of these terms in the glossary at the end of the book as well. The goal of these glossary sections is not just to help define terms you may be a little unsure of, but also to help clear up the misconceptions about these terms and what they actually mean for our discussion.

Close (or Closing): refers to when a real estate transaction between a buyer and seller is finalized. The documents related to the conveying of title are executed by all parties. This usually takes place at a title company. Once everything is executed and approved (if an approval is required by a lender) the transaction can be funded. Funding occurs when money changes hands.

Earnest Money: This is a monetary deposit made payable to the title company facilitating the transaction that shows the buyer's good faith in the contract that was executed between both parties.

For example, Joe put down $2,000 earnest money in his contract with Tom and sent it to American Title for them to hold. If you do not close the transaction as the buyer, your earnest money can be refundable or non-refundable depending on how the contract was written. If you do close the transaction, your earnest money is credited towards the purchase price.

FSBO (For Sale By Owner): This is when a seller sells a property without the assistance of an agent or broker.

Market Appreciation: This is when the value of a property increases due to positive changes in the market.

Memorandum of Contract: This is a document that gets recorded in the county of record that states that a buyer has a contract with a seller for a specific property address that was executed on a specific date. This document becomes a public record, allowing title companies to find it and prevent a closing on a property that is under contract with another party.

For example, Bob (the buyer) gets a property under contract with Susan (the seller), and records his interest in their contract with a memorandum of contract. Bob, as the executor of the memorandum, believes he has a great deal that he negotiated and does not want Susan to go around him and sell to someone else. This document can prevent Susan from doing this and gives Bob legal recourse if she does.

MLS (Multiple Listing Service): The MLS is a private database managed by real estate professionals to help connect brokers who have clients looking to buy with brokers who have clients looking to sell. The majority of properties for sale in a given market are often listed by brokers on their respective MLS. Sellers of property are under a listing agreement with the broker allowing them to disseminate information about the property that other brokers and users of the system can access.

Listings on the MLS typically include (but are not limited to) the property address, a description of the property, number of bedrooms, baths, square footage, year built, school district, days on market, listing broker contact information, etc.

I typically refer to properties listed for sale on the MLS as "on market," and those that are not on the MLS as "off-market." You will see these terms used at different points in this text.

Option Fee: For purposes of this book, it means a monetary amount made payable to a seller from a buyer for consideration to have the opportunity to terminate a contract between them for any reason within a specified period of time.

For example, Paul (the buyer) gave John (the seller) a $200 option check in exchange for ten days to decide if he wants to move forward with the transaction. This is also referred to as the option period or inspection period since this is when properties are inspected. Option fees are generally non-refundable, and are credited toward the purchase price if you do close the transaction.

Seller Concessions: Contributions made to a buyer at the time of closing to pay for closing costs and costs related to the buyer's financing. It is basically a gift from the seller to the buyer, which effectively lowers the purchase price of the property.

This is an important term to understand because it impacts the actual sales price of the property when the property becomes a sold comparable. This means if a property is sold for $100,000 and had $5,000 in seller concessions, the actual sales price is $95,000 because the concessions are factored into the equation. Many appraisers will view this sold comparable as selling for $95,000 and not $100,000.

Title Company: A title company is a neutral third party that assists in the conveyance (the transfer) of ownership between sellers and buyers of real property. Title companies make sure that the title (ownership) to a given property is legitimate and offer insurance on the title through a title insurance policy to the buyer and also to a lender through what is called a mortgagee's title policy, if the property is going to be financed. This ensures that there are no other claims against the property, for example, by other family members or heirs, or by vendors who may not have been paid by a prior owner of the property for work performed.

Total Acquisition Cost: The formula for this is:
Purchase Price + Rehab Amount (Scope of Work) + Closing Costs = Total Acquisition Cost

CHAPTER 6

THE DEAL

The word *deal* is thrown around a lot in this book as well as in the investing world. You will hear investors say, "Is it a deal?" or "This deal does not work for me," or "Bring me something that is a better deal." What does this mean, and what do we mean by the term "deal"?

For our purposes, the term means a couple of things. One, a deal is first and foremost the property itself (a.k.a. the subject property). Two, it also refers to what you or another investor are willing to pay for a given property based on the formulas we are going to cover for each of the investing strategies. So, what you might think is a "deal" for you can be much different than what someone else is willing to pay for it.

Wholesaling, flipping, and even buying rental property, can be confusing topics to understand, especially if you are brand new to the business. To make it easier, I have included a story to help us get started with this section.

A Story About How Deals Happen

One day while sitting at my desk, I get a call from a man named John who received a "We Buy Houses" post card from me in the mail. During the call, John mentioned that he inherited a house from his mother who had passed away, and didn't want to deal with the hassle of hiring a real estate agent to sell it. He also informed me that the house needed a lot of repairs, had been vacant for three years, and since he lived out of town, he had no way of dealing with the situation.

John unfortunately had lost his job six months ago and was going to be evicted from his apartment if he didn't get some money quickly. When he saw that the post card said we would buy houses in any condition, pay cash and close fast, he decided to call. He gave me permission to access the property and I went over that same day, after I determined what the potential value was for this deal.

The house was in very bad shape. While walking up to the front door I noticed the roof was worn way past its functional life, one of the front windows was broken, and most of the yard was filled with weeds two feet tall. The bricks had stair step cracks along the wall, showing evidence of some foundation problems. When I entered the house, the smell was awful. In fact, you could smell something bad while walking up the driveway.

The house was filled with furniture, as well as boxes stacked from floor to ceiling in every room. This was no doubt a hoarder house. The kitchen was in shambles with the cabinets literally falling off the walls. The ceiling was leaking and there was water damage throughout the interior. I think you get the idea. This place was a total wreck and was going to need a lot of work in order to make it livable again. I took several photos, made some notes, and went back to my office to crunch the numbers.

This house could fit any investing strategy I wanted to take: wholesale it, flip it, or keep it as a rental. The after repair value was $150,000. The cost to completely rehab the house was around $50,000, and my offer to John was $45,000. Now you might be thinking, "there is absolutely no way he is going to sell it for that low of a price." You're correct. We settled on $47,000. Hey, don't be surprised. These types of deals do happen, and the more time you spend in this business, the more deals like this you are going to see.

At this point, you probably have some questions about many of the things I mentioned. What does after repair value mean? How did you determine the total cost for the scope of work? And how did you get the seller to take a price of $47,000? These are great questions and I will answer them as we progress through the book.

You may also want to know what I did with this particular deal. Well, I sold it wholesale it to another investor for $62,000. Wholesaling is the first investing strategy that we are going to discuss, because it's the easiest one to implement when getting started.

CHAPTER 7

WHOLESALING

The concept behind selling a property wholesale is exactly the same as the concept of buying and selling wholesale with any other product. In this case, the product is a house. It would be contracted by you from the owner of record (the seller) at a price low enough for you to be able to sell it at a higher price to someone else.

THE BENEFITS OF AN IMMEDIATE INCOME STRATEGY

Wholesaling is an *immediate income strategy,* meaning you do not do any significant work to the property before you sell it. In some cases, you can close in as little as a week or as soon as the title work is ready. Wholesaling can also be one of the least expensive ways to get into real estate investing in terms of finding deals, and one of the best ways to learn the business.

To be successful in real estate investing, you need to have the ability to move a deal quickly to someone whether you are looking to make a quick assignment fee (which we will discuss shortly) or just move a deal you are not interested in doing yourself. Wholesaling will allow you to do both of these. It is important that you understand this as you are evaluating a deal. There are a couple of key points to keep in mind here:

1. **Wholesale deals are not rehabbed in any way.** However, it may make sense for you to do a trash out and/or cleanup of the property to get the maximum amount from the sale. It's not necessary to do any tangible improvements to the property because you are offering this deal at a discount and your buyer is going to do the heavy lifting.

2. **Houses in every price range can be wholesaled.** However, it is a function of the market you are in that will determine the best range for you to target. Generally, the lower the value, the easier it is to sell/wholesale, since there are more available buyers and investing strategies. If you contract it at the right price, almost any house can be moved to a wholesale buyer.

Now that you understand how wholesaling is different from flipping, we need to talk a little bit about the different ways that wholesaling can work. Depending on the laws in your state, as well as the opportunity you have in question, you will need to decide if it makes more sense for you to assign your contract to a buyer or purchase for a double closing.

ASSIGNING CONTRACTS

Assigning a contract means transferring a binding agreement that you have between yourself and the seller/owner of record, to another buyer. Using this technique, you never actually purchase the property, and title is never transferred/conveyed to you.

It's as simple as it sounds, but there are some nuances depending on where you live and the type of seller involved in the transaction. Real estate laws differ in each state, and of course there are federal laws that trump state law. You will need to verify if your state allows you to assign a contract without having a real estate license. For instance, at the time of this writing, no license is required in Texas. Also, you will need to find a title company that will allow you to close with an assignment of contract (more on this shortly).

Either way, the process of assigning your contract involves creating an Assignment of Contract document that will allow you to transfer/sell your contract to another party for a fee (usually collected at closing) called an **assignment fee**. This assignment fee is how you make money in the transaction.

Why Assign a Contract?

There are two documents involved in an assignment of contract transaction: the contract between you and the seller, and the assignment of contract between you and your buyer. There are also some reasons why you would assign a contract instead of double closing:

1. **There is no money required from you to close the transaction**. That's right. Your buyer is bringing money to closing, not you, since they have assumed everything in your contract by executing the Assignment of Contract. Your assignment fee is simply added by the title company to the settlement statement at closing. When your buyer and seller close the transaction (both have signed the appropriate documents to convey title), and it has been funded (meaning money has changed hands and been transferred from your buyer to the seller), you will receive your assignment fee, usually via check or wire transfer.

2. **Assigning a contract can be a simpler way to close**. It's one transaction as opposed to two. Two transactions require some additional coordination, since there are more people involved. In most cases, you can make your money faster by assigning a contract instead of double closing.

3. **You trust that your buyer will purchase the property.** Your buyer is solid and has given you or

the title company a check for earnest money or option money. I strongly advise you to make sure your buyer has "skin in the game" money down, either to you or the title company, so you can ensure they are going to close on the contract that you assigned to them. If your buyer walks away from the deal, your assignment of contract should have a clause permitting you to keep this money.

4. **You believe in the seller's commitment**. Your seller is committed to closing and conveying the title as they agreed in the contract. If there are some reservations here, be sure to read my section at the end of this chapter regarding *Memorandums of Contract.*

DOUBLE CLOSING

Yes, you have another option that can be very effective: purchase the property and sell it to your buyer, or list it on the MLS as an "investor special." Here you would have a contract between you and the seller/owner of record with the intent of closing on the purchase and taking title to the property. You will actually own the property, however, just for a short period of time until you sell it.

This option is called double closing; the property is sold and title transferred twice. The actual timeframe between your purchase and your sale in a double close can vary. It can be immediate (on the same day), or it can take a week or more.

Why Double Close?

Wouldn't it be easier to just assign it as we illustrated in the above section and get the exact fee you are looking to make? Not necessarily. In fact, you can make more money double closing than by merely assigning the contract.

Here are some reasons to purchase the property and then sell it via a double close:

1. **The seller needs money quickly.** Controlling the situation is critical, especially when you are dealing with a motivated seller who needs money. If you have a seller who needs to get their money faster than you can find a buyer, you need to double close.

   Some sellers will not be honorable, and will go around you and your contract and sell it to someone else who may pay slightly more. What! Yes, it has happened to me, and I learned my lesson a long time ago. I have seen it happen to many of my real estate investor friends as well.

   Once you have the deal under contract, sellers sometimes get what I call "sellers' remorse." They begin to think, "I could have gotten more for this house," or "That buyer ripped me off." This doesn't take away from the fact that if both of you agreed to a deal in writing, it's a binding contract.

   Given the laws in your state, you may need to seek the appropriate recourse if a seller were to go around you and get under contract with someone else. Don't think this can happen?

   Hey, it's natural for someone to think they could have gotten a higher offer. Have you ever sold something and thought, "If I had been more patient, I probably could have sold it for more money?" Some sellers you will be working with are not professional sales or business people. They just need money and/ or need to get out of their situation quickly. They don't want to deal with a real estate agent or spend time and money trying to sell their house.

   I am telling you all of this because I want you to think like the seller when you are getting the deal under contract. When you are thinking like a seller and empathizing with their situation, you are going to make them feel very comfortable working with you, respect what they tell you and honor your end of the deal.

2. **Owning the property gives you more control over the deal**. You will have more time to market it and potentially get a higher price because you are not under any pressure from the seller who calls you every day wanting to know when they are going to get their money. I would say that some of my best wholesale deals were purchased first and then immediately listed on the MLS as an "investor special" for all cash. Doing this gives you great market exposure allowing real estate agents and investors in that market the ability to see your deal.

3. **Some title companies will not close an assignment of contract**. For whatever reason, there are some title companies that do not like to close transactions that have an assignment of contract. There may be legal reasons (different by state), insurance underwriting reasons, or just company policy why they won't close them.

4. **Bank foreclosures are not allowed to be assigned**. If this is a bank REO (real estate owned by the bank, a.k.a. foreclosure) you will not be allowed to assign this. Why? Banks will not allow assignments, at least not as of this writing, and require you, the buyer on the contract, to close. Maybe this will change at some point, but I have not seen a bank or financial institution ever allow a contract to be assigned in a single-family situation.

If you are in a situation where you don't have the money to purchase a deal for cash, don't worry about it. If the deal is good enough, you can use hard money (a topic we will discuss later) or some other type of private loan. Just get the deal done!

Don't Be Afraid to Seek Legal Advice

If you are confused by this discussion, and don't have the necessary documentation to facilitate this type of transaction (i.e., an Assignment of Contract), or don't know if you need to be licensed in your area in order to assign contracts, then *get with a real estate attorney* to help you with this.

Before you hire an attorney to create the correct assignment of contract document for you, make sure you understand how to complete a real estate contract with the seller, because you may need your attorney's help to do this (or certainly the help of a real estate agent or broker).

Working With Title Companies

Once the contract between you and the seller/owner of record is executed, you need to send it to the title company that will facilitate the closing of this transaction. The contract should contain a place to insert the name of the title company that is to be utilized in the fastest timeframe possible. But before you can send the contract over to the title company, you need to know which title company to use. You are going to need to find an *investor friendly* title company that can handle an assignment and/or a double close.

How do you find this type of title company? Ask the members of your mastermind group. Don't have a mastermind group yet? Find a title company by networking at a local meetup group, or some local real estate investor organization. Someone will be there who can recommend an investor friendly title company. Or in the worst case, just call different title companies until you find one that will work for you.

If you are going to be a real estate investor, it's important that you find a title company where you can conduct business. Not every title company likes the investor space because investor deals are generally smaller and require a volume of business to make money. Investor deals can also be complicated with divorce situations, deaths and probate, as well as the heirship issues that go along with that (meaning who is actually entitled to sell the property). Also, investor deals can suck up a lot of time and resources, and there are title companies that just won't touch any contract that is being assigned.

Once you have determined the title company you will work with, the next step is to send the contract over to them with your earnest money.

A Wholesale Scenario

So, let's consider another scenario and determine whether or not it represents a good wholesale deal to assign:

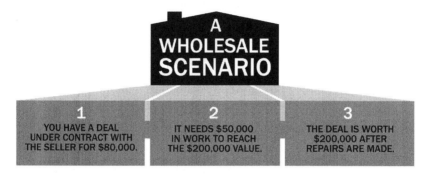

If you find a deal like this, great job! This is an incredible deal here! Remember, in wholesaling, your goal is to *maximize your profit* without doing any work to the house. You should be very confident that you can sell your contract for $10,000. How do I know this? Most investors, both new and experienced, will buy a deal that has 30% equity built in, after the repairs are considered.

We will discuss this in more detail in the next chapter, but in the example above, the purchase price plus repairs is $130,000. With an assignment fee of $10,000, that puts the effective cost to your buyer at $140,000 (most investors do not include closing costs as part of this calculation). This gives you 30% equity (or 30% X $200,000 which is $60,000).

The reality is someone will pay more for this deal. If you have the ability to hold out for more, you should absolutely do it. I have seen investors pay up to $185,000 for a deal like this. Personally, I would never do that. But there are investors who will.

For our purposes here, selling at $140,000 would be a great deal for you and your buyer because there will be a lot of immediate buyers for it at this price. Now all you have to do is find them, which you can do with some online resources, at a local real estate investor club or Meetup group, or better yet, someone from your mastermind group. If you present this deal at your next meeting, or by emailing your group, you will have no issues moving this deal. In fact, that would be where I would start if I wanted to be sure I got the deal done.

Once you get some experience and make more connections, you will be able to move this deal at an even higher price to someone else.

RECORDING YOUR INTEREST WITH A MEMORANDUM OF CONTRACT

As I mentioned in the preceding paragraphs, you always want to be in control of your deal throughout the process. I also want to emphasize that having sellers going around you and getting under contract with another buyer can be a real issue. You need to be paranoid about this because if you are not, it's going to happen to you at some point.

How can you prevent it? Well, you cannot prevent someone from breaching your contract, but you can potentially prevent a seller from closing with another buyer with what is called a *Memorandum of Contract.*

In the real estate world, contracts are not recorded in the public records. However, you can put the world on notice by recording a Memorandum of Contract, which basically states that the named buyer and the named seller have a contract on a property as of a specific date for a specific property address and legal description. I have recorded many Memorandums of Contract on many deals. It really doesn't matter if you are going to wholesale it, flip it, or keep it as a rental. Many times, you will not know right away what you are going to do with the property. You just know it's a good deal and you don't want it to go to someone else.

The Memorandum of Contract is signed and notarized by you as the buyer and then recorded in the county/public records. When a title company does its abstract search in the public records it should find this document showing the property is/was under contract. I say "should" because sometimes title companies miss things, which is why you get title insurance on every deal you are buying!

51

If a title company sees that the buyer on the contract is not the buyer on the Memorandum of Contract, it should not close that transaction until the memorandum has been released. This happens through a Release of Memorandum of Contract. If a seller has gone around you in a contract, you may require them to pay you to release it.

As always, seek out an attorney to help you (especially one at a title company). Be sure to record it quickly. If the seller tries to close, the title company will see it (hopefully) and stop the sale.

I have had friends get called from the title company saying there is a memorandum recorded with their name on it, and asked them to release it so the transaction could be closed. My friends were able to force the seller to pay them to terminate their contract and release the memorandum. It's definitely an effective tool.

CHAPTER 8

FLIPPING PROPERTY

Flipping property is one of the best ways to make large profits in real estate. If you want to quickly turn a profit in real estate investing, then flipping property should be your focus. Flipping in most cases, but certainly not all, produces a higher return than wholesaling.

Flipping can also be one of the best ways to lose a lot of money in real estate. I have seen more investors lose money when they deviated from what they were told to do by their hard money lender, by their contractor, or by the appraiser who assessed the property in the beginning.

You have to know your numbers in every deal. By that I mean the actual numbers and not some estimate or what you "think" the after-repair value will be. This is covered in depth in Section Three: Due Diligence.

Compared to the other investing strategies, flipping is the riskiest due to the fact that you are carrying a vacant property for the period of time needed to complete the necessary improvements to make it market ready. There are unknowns that pop up all the time when you rehab a property that can impact your profit.

Also, the amount of time it takes for you to complete the work impacts your profit. The longer you take, the more it costs you in terms of any carrying costs you may have.

However, with risk comes reward. If you do everything correctly, you will maximize the amount of profit you can get from the deal versus a wholesale strategy and certainly any rental cash flow.

The concept behind flipping is to buy the property at a discount to the after-repaired market value, complete all of the necessary repairs/improvements, and sell it for a retail price in a short timeframe.

A short timeframe for me is 120 days. This means have the property sold to another buyer on or before 120 days from your purchase date. If I don't think I can sell the property within that timeframe, I would probably re-evaluate the deal. Now, this doesn't mean I wouldn't do the deal, it just means I need to determine why it's going to take longer to sell. It could be a function of the market, the scope of work required, or something else. I would want to understand what this is before getting under contract to buy, to make sure I was purchasing it at the right price. And to make sure we purchase it at the right price, we need to focus on using the right formula.

FORMULA FOR SUCCESS

Unlike wholesaling, flipping property and making a comfortable profit requires you to have a certain amount of equity in the deal for the numbers to work. Luckily for all of us, someone figured out the formula, and it has become an industry standard for buying property that you are going to flip. You may already know the formula, but in case you don't, it is:

ARV × 70% MINUS (-) REPAIRS = MAO

ARV is the After Repair Value. This means the value that the property would appraise and/or sell for after the tangible improvements have been completed. In other words, you buy the property, complete the scope of work (all of the necessary repairs), and now you have improved it to market value.

The ARV is then multiplied by 70%. The repairs are then subtracted, leaving you with the **MAO** (pronounced mā-ō), which is the Maximum Allowable Offer you should make to a given seller.

Let's take a look at an example:

- A house has an ARV of $100,000.

- It needs $20,000 in work.

- What is the MAO? $100,000 X .7 - $20,000 = $50,000

What is the most you should buy this house for to make an acceptable profit? The answer is **no more than $50,000.** If you buy it for $50,000 or less, then you are purchasing the deal at the appropriate price.

Now, you might be saying, "I can still make a nice profit if I buy it for $55,000." True, you probably can. However, if you are new in this business and have never flipped a house before, I would encourage you NOT to do this. Your risk goes up significantly the more you deviate from the formula.

At this point you might be wondering what the actual profit is if you purchased it for $50,000. Before you look at the answer below, try to calculate what you think the profit might be. Most new investors I encounter overestimate the profit by a significant amount, so don't worry if you happen to do the same thing.

Do you think you have it now? The average net profit in a house in this example is $13,500. If you thought it was higher, you are not alone. The gross profit is $30,000, but to calculate the net profit you have to consider other costs.

FIVE COSTS INVESTORS TYPICALLY FORGET

Now that we know the margins on flipping are slimmer than what most beginning real estate investors assume, let's talk for a minute about why this percentage is so low, why new investors often get this wrong, and why the net profit in the prior example is only $13,500.

The reason new investors think there is more money in a deal is that they are incorrectly calculating their net profit. This often happens because they are basing their numbers off the *gross profit,* and leaving out one or more of the costs we are about to address. Wholesalers contribute to this overestimation because they love to advertise their deals with a gross profit number, which is always higher than what an investor will actually net. It's even worse when the house has a higher ARV because the dollar amounts are larger and can be deceiving if you are not focusing on the actual equity percentage.

So pay close attention to the following information. There are five costs incurred at the sale of a property that go into another formula we will use to calculate the net profit. These costs are:

1. **Seller's Closing Costs**: This includes the title company escrow fees, title insurance, recording fees, and any other title company costs.

2. **Carrying Costs**: This would include utilities expenses such as water, gas and electric, as well as any interest expense if you borrowed money to purchase the property.

3. **Seller Concessions**: If your buyer doesn't have enough money to bring to closing, they can ask you, the seller, for some assistance. This assistance means they want you to pay for some of their closing costs and/or lender costs. Only certain loans are eligible for this type of assistance, and it effectively lowers your sales price.

   For example, you sell a house for $100,000. Let's say the buyer's closing costs are $4,000 (or 4% of the purchase price), but they don't have $4,000. They only have $2,000. They ask you in the contract to offer a seller concession of 2%. If you agree, and the deal closes, you effectively sold them the house for $98,000.

   Seller concessions are only allowed in certain loans since they must be approved by the lender. As of today, all federally backed mortgage loans allow for some seller concessions up to a specific loan amount. It's up to you as the seller to accept them or not.

4. **Commissions**: If you are listing the house on the MLS (which you should be doing), you are going to have to pay your agent or broker a commission. In most markets, six percent is the norm.

5. **Pro-rated Property Taxes**: As a seller, you will have to credit the property taxes to the buyer for the current year up to the date of closing on the sale. So if you sold the property on May 31, you would have to credit exactly five months' worth of property taxes to the buyer at the sale closing.

To calculate the actual net profit you will make in any deal where you intend to flip the property, you need to use the following formula:

FINAL SALE PRICE — MINUS (-) YOUR PURCHASE PRICE — MINUS (-) PURCHASE CLOSING COSTS — MINUS (-) REPAIRS — MINUS (-) 5 COSTS INVESTORS FORGET

= **NET PROFIT**

To summarize, it is important for you to determine what constitutes a deal for you—what gets you to your anticipated net profit. If you are looking to make no less than $20,000 net profit on every deal, then you are going to need to find deals that have an ARV of something greater than $100,000. Why? Because as we mentioned above, the net profit in a deal that size is generally only $13,500, unless you buy it way below 70% minus repairs.

BUILDING THE REST OF YOUR TEAM

To make consistent profits that are in line with your expectations and not based on guesswork, it's important to continue adding the best resources to your team. In Chapter 1, I mentioned using attorneys to get legal advice. In Chapter 4, I discussed the power of a mastermind group and how essential it is for you to create a team of people around you with like interests to further your success. There are two other additions to your team that are fundamental to having success especially in flipping: a good contractor and a good real estate agent/broker.

Why mention this here? Don't you need to have a good contractor and a good real estate agent/broker when you are wholesaling? What about when you are buying rental properties?

These are very good questions, and the answer is quite possibly, "Yes." There is a point during the deal qualification process when you will want to engage your agent/broker and your contractor. However, you need these resources even more so when you are flipping property, so I wanted this to be the point where I introduce them and their benefits.

Contractors

Contractors sometime get a bad rap, and unfortunately, many of the stereotypes about them are true. However, not all of them are the same, and the great ones are out there, and they are reasonably priced. Keep in mind that it's better to pay someone more to do the job correctly the first time than have to hire someone else to fix something that you already paid to repair.

What a Good Contractor Can Do for You

When it comes to contracting work, there are three things we all want: **good, fast and cheap.**

There's also an old saying with real estate investors, "You can have any two of these." For those of you who don't quite get it, this means if you want fast and cheap, the quality of the work is probably going to suffer. If you want good and cheap, it's going to take a longer time to complete the project. If you want good and fast, it's probably going to be expensive.

Many real estate investors (including myself) want to keep costs to a minimum. It's natural to do this no matter how big or small the project. However, it's important to keep in mind what you are ultimately trying to accomplish based on your investing strategy, so you can determine the level of work the project is going to require.

For example, if you are keeping the property as a rental, you may not require the same finish out as you would with a property you are flipping. If you are wholesaling the property, you may need to get an estimate for both rent-ready and full retail sale because your sale price is going to reflect the work required.

Once you know what you are going to do with a particular deal, you can get the appropriate contractor(s) to help you estimate the scope of work. Most do not charge for this, but want to get the business. Keep this in mind so you don't overuse someone. If you decide to wholesale full time and are not quite comfortable estimating a scope of work, you will need to work with someone that you can pay (a nominal amount) to work up a bid for you.

The Key Traits and Behaviors of a Good Contractor

A good contractor, in my opinion and for purposes of this book, is someone who:

1. Is full time in their line of business (i.e., general contractor, electrician, plumber, foundation repair, HVAC, etc.)

2. Has several years of experience (5+)

3. Is conscious of the needs of his/her client

4. Can effectively manage their money (or has someone do this for them)

5. Has the ability to assess a real estate investor's needs and can quickly put together the correct repair estimate or scope of work

6. Can manage their client's expectations

7. Above all else, is honest

I know that sounds like a lot to ask for, but such contractors are out there, and you need to find them. A contractor who meets these criteria is one who can give you an accurate assessment of the scope of work needed, along with the cost, and do so in a timely manner.

Once you find this contractor, they need to be added to your team, and you need to find two backups/replacements for them. I know, it sounds like a lot of work, but it's really not, and it is absolutely worth it. Why, you ask? Because inevitably, that contractor (especially if they are good) is not going to be available when you need them. Sometimes deals move fast, and you need an answer right away. You may not have time to get that particular contractor to the property.

Also, contractors can go bad. There may be changes to the people on their team, they may get overextended, or something else may prevent them from either showing up or doing a good job on your project. I have experienced this more than a few times. You will be using your contractor on the first couple of deals and everything goes great. Then on the next one, they completely screw it up! You get sideways with your contractor and decide–no more! Hopefully, you won't experience this too many times before you find the right ones.

Once you get to a point where you have experience and have some projects under your belt, you will be able to keep solid, consistent contractors busy enough that they will take your call. And make sure to pay your contractors on time. You will then have added a key member to your team, and be on your way to having success.

Real Estate Agents and Brokers

There are some terms that are used interchangeably in this book. It's important to note how I am using these terms in this section and throughout the text. Those terms are *Real Estate Agent* and *Real Estate Broker*. When I refer to an *agent*, I mean someone who is licensed, works for a *broker*, and is working one-on-one with you as a seller or buyer of real property.

When I refer to a broker, I mean someone who has licensed real estate agents working under their broker license. They may also perform the duties of a real estate agent.

Whatever your opinion is of real estate agents and/or brokers, I think you need to read the rest of this section to put everything into perspective. I am not trying to insinuate anything here. Like contractors, you may have had positive or negative experiences with agents and brokers. I just want to make sure you understand their value and what to look for when trying to find a good one.

The Value of a Good Real Estate Agent

Now, I want to make a case for using a good real estate agent and making them a key member of your team. The first thing you have to know about real estate agents is not all of them are created equal. Many years ago, I heard a broker with 40 years of experience say, "Of all the licensed real estate agents in the market, only 1% of them are actually any good."

If you've had an experience with one of the many no-good real estate agents/brokers out there, I want you to understand it doesn't have to be like that. You just need to find a good one, which I want to help you do. I realize the term "good" is very subjective, so I want to qualify what I mean here.

What to Look for in a "Good" Real Estate Agent

I got lucky. The first real estate agent I met called me off one of my For Sale By Owner signs in front of a house I was selling. I actually had many agents call me off the sign, but this one was different, and in ten seconds, I knew I could work with her.

She immediately told me that she had a buyer for my house and asked if I would pay her a commission. I agreed and we ended up working together for several years until she left the business. She delivered value by keeping buyers in line, and she focused on getting deals closed. From working with her and other good real estate agents, I've learned what to look for:

When you find someone like this, be sure to hang on to them for as long as possible.

FOR SALE BY OWNER

The more time you spend in real estate, the more you will see things and wonder if they make sense or not. One of those is certainly the decision to list your property on the MLS with a broker or go the other route: For Sale by Owner (FSBO).

When I was getting started, I thought FSBO was a great way to market a property, and I didn't see any value in using a real estate agent. At the time, I didn't think it made sense to pay someone a commission just to list a property. I have a sales background, so why would I let someone else sell my property when I can do that myself. Once again, this was one of the things I learned the hard way.

Many of the first deals I sold were FSBO, which tainted my thinking even more. This was with some rentals that had been owned for a while, and it was during a time when financing was becoming easier to obtain. You are likely very familiar with the story of subprime lending and the subsequent mortgage crisis that followed. This made selling to tenants customary. If you didn't sell to a tenant who was looking to buy, they were eventually going to vacate because they had seen their friends, neighbors, and co-workers get mortgages, and they too wanted the dream of home ownership.

Three reasons why selling FSBO is a mistake:

1. Limits your market exposure
2. Taints the market's perception of you and your property
3. Costs you more than hiring a real estate agent

Limits Exposure

Think this through with me: If your property is not on the MLS, it is receiving ZERO market exposure from every other broker/agent in town. If all you have is a sign in the front yard, you only get local traffic. No exposure means no buyers. Why would you limit yourself to such a small buyer pool? Even if you paid too much for this deal, or repairs spiraled out of control and you are going to lose money, you still need to move the property off your books as quickly as possible. The fastest way is with an agent/broker listed on the MLS.

Taints Your Property

There are two things going on here with regard to perception. First, they perceive you as being cheap and unwilling to pay a real estate commission. Whether that is true or not, that's what is going to be perceived. This will certainly prevent many agents from even showing your property to one of their clients. They know they are going to have to deal with you personally, and they will have to negotiate some form of compensation/ commission with you.

Second, if the asking price for the property is higher than the average sales price for the area, and/or is in an area that is more affluent, the perception will be that your property is not worth it. But you just spent $20K on the hardwood flooring, $18K on the custom cabinets, and $15K on the appliances. You put travertine in the kitchen and baths, modern chrome fixtures, and a number of other upgrades. No one knows this because they would have to call you to get the info. You are asking $750,000 for this house on the same street as another house that is listed with a local, brand-named brokerage sign, who also has a stellar reputation. That house has a description of the same things in yours, but theirs is on every real estate site on the Internet. When buyers drive by, they see the $3 sign you bought from Home Depot that says, "For Sale By Owner," with your phone number scratched in the white space at the bottom. They won't be motivated to stop or call you.

If you think that all an agent does is enter the property address and description in the MLS, and then waits for the deal to close so they can get a commission, you are absolutely mistaken. If that's all your current agent does, it's time to find a good one. I can personally guarantee you this will make all the difference in your ability to make money flipping properties.

Costs You More

In most cases, you are going to have to pay someone a commission to bring you a buyer because most homes are sold by agents/brokers. Also, in most cases, FSBO is going to keep your property on the market for a much longer period of time. The longer it stays on the market, the more interest, utilities, and property taxes you pay, along with the more landscaping you have to maintain. If you don't have any experience working with buyers, you may end up going with someone who is not really approved for financing, wasting even more time. It's much safer and faster to list the property on the MLS, and it will certainly be more profitable.

MAKING THAT FIRST OFFER WORK

Now, one more thing fundamental when flipping houses is *making the first offer work*. If you haven't been through this yet, I want you to think through the following scenario with me. It's a little detailed, but it will make sense:

- Your contractor is finished remodeling your house, and they do an amazing job.

- It takes a little bit longer than you would have liked (but what deal doesn't?).

- After 60 days, you finally have the house on the market. You correctly decided to list it on the MLS to get maximum market exposure.

- You list it on a Thursday afternoon to attract the most buyers from the coming weekend.

- You get three showings on Friday and four on Saturday. Now this is great because a high number of showings is a strong indicator you've priced the property correctly.

- On Sunday, your agent informs you that you have two offers:

  ◦ One is a low-ball, investor offer.

  ◦ The other is a full price offer for $200,000 with no concessions.

- Obviously you'd reject the low-ball offer, but the full-price offer sounds great, right?

- Next, your agent verifies that the buyer is approved for financing and that they are actually putting 20% down, with 1% earnest money and a $200 option fee for seven days.

- You accept the offer and are now officially under contract.

- The option period starts and the inspection is taking place in a couple of days.

- You finally get a copy of the buyer's inspection report and discover:

  ◦ The electrical panel is a Federal Pacific and the inspector flags it as a known fire hazard.

  ◦ The hot water heater doesn't have a pan underneath it.

  ◦ The roof has hail damage that wasn't discovered during your initial walk through.

- ◦ Multiple other little things that were not part of the code requirements when the house was built are discovered.

- Suddenly, the buyer is scared because this is their first home, and they want everything to be repaired/replaced.

I know what you are thinking (minus expletives), because I have been there many times. "There is no way I am going to agree to this! I just spent $45,000 rehabbing this house, and I'm not spending another dollar on it." Well, I totally understand. But, what I want you to realize is that you really need to try to make that first offer work, which is another reason why a good real estate agent is so valuable.

Depend On Your Real Estate Agent

If you get into a situation like this where you feel yourself becoming angry, an experienced real estate agent can take over and negotiate for you and keep you at a safe distance from the buyer. If your agent is a good negotiator, they can try to have some of these things removed from the buyer's list.

Compare this to dealing with the buyer's agent directly where it may be difficult for you to maintain your composure. You don't want to lose your temper, say the wrong thing, and blow up your deal thinking, "Who cares about this offer? There are more buyers out there, and this is a hot market! I'm telling them NO to everything!" If this is your attitude, you are making a big mistake, and here is why:

Your First Offer Is Likely the Best

Statistically (and commonly known among brokers and agents) *your first offer is likely the best offer you are going to get*. Now of course this isn't always the case because there are no absolutes in anything. However, if you have given the property adequate market exposure, and had a number of showings with one or more offers (especially a full-price offer), there is a very strong possibility this is the best offer you'll ever get.

In fact, if everything checks out with the buyer (approval letter, earnest money, and option fee), you more than likely have a solid offer. If you don't get the sense that this buyer is solid, and something is telling you that they will be difficult, by all means, decline the offer and wait for the right one.

Don't Assume the Buyer is Trying to Be Difficult

Another thing to keep in mind is just because the buyer wants all of these inspection items resolved, doesn't necessarily mean they are being difficult. This is a normal part of the negotiating process. In fact, if the big items (bad electrical panels and/or a damaged roof) are not addressed, you are more than likely going to have to deal with this with the next buyer on their inspection.

Once your property is under contract, the status changes on the MLS and there is a history with your property. If you don't close, the status is going to change back to Active again, potentially raising questions among other agents as to whether there is something wrong with the property.

What Repairs Should You Make?

In the previous scenario, I would probably agree to replace the panel, install a new roof, and negotiate the other items off the list through my agent. This is very reasonable based on my experience. You are not giving in to everything, but you are focusing on the most important items that are going to come up again and impact the next buyer. If the buyer agrees to this, you are more than likely good through closing. If they do not, you may be forced to move on to another buyer.

The point is *keep your emotions in check and focus on your main objective* which is to get the property sold, make money, and move on to the next deal. No two situations are the same, and there is no way to document every scenario that you will encounter. If you are on your first deal or fifty-first deal, my advice is to use an experienced agent for all of your sales transactions. I am speaking from experience because it has worked well for me over time.

Remember, Time Is Elapsing

There is something else going on here: time is elapsing. Even though your Days on Market stops once you are under contract, time is elapsing, and that is costing you money. Remember, once you close on the purchase, the clock starts ticking. It's ticking on any interest or utilities you are paying, and on pro-rated taxes that you have to credit to your buyer at closing for the time you owned the property. It may also be ticking on that ideal time of year during which you want to market the property.

The longer you take to sell the property, the more pressure there is for you to adjust your price. If you don't lower your price after a certain amount of time, you will probably see an offer that comes in lower because that buyer sees you've had it listed for a while and it's still active. When they see this, it can prompt them to send a lower offer your way. Also, they see that there was some activity but now it's back on the market. All this hurts your ability to maximize your return.

If you cannot come to terms with the first buyer on what is going to be fixed, and they decide to terminate (remember the buyer, in most cases, is the only one that can legally terminate the contract, and they must do so during the option period), it may be a while before you get another offer. Depending on market conditions, your property may look tainted and showings can come to a screeching halt. So do your best to make that first offer work.

CHAPTER 9

RENTAL PROPERTY

Wholesaling and flipping property are fundamental strategies to consider whenever you are evaluating a potential deal. However, if the spread in the deal you find is too thin to wholesale or flip (meaning there is not enough equity in the deal to make money with either option), you may want to consider rehabbing the property (if required) and holding it as a rental.

I can just hear many of you saying, "I never want to own rental property because I don't want to get called at 3:00 AM from a tenant because their AC isn't working." I get it. Just know that anyone who takes calls at 3:00 AM has not properly trained their tenants! Also, you don't need to take any tenant calls ever if you can hire a good property manager to handle this for you (more on this later).

THE BENEFITS OF OWNING RENTAL PROPERTY

Don't let any of those tenant stories prevent you from buying rental properties. In my opinion, owning rental property is the single greatest wealth-building investment vehicle. As I stated earlier, what other investment vehicle pays you so many ways:

5 WAYS TO GET PAID

CASH FLOW
THE INCOME GENERATED FROM RENT AFTER SUBTRACTING PRINCIPAL, INTEREST, TAXES AND INSURANCE

EQUITY
THE DIFFERENCE BETWEEN THE PROPERTY VALUE AND YOUR TOTAL COST OF PURCHASE (I.E., PURCHASE PRICE + REPAIRS)

APPRECIATION
ALTHOUGH YOU MAKE YOUR MONEY WHEN YOU BUY REAL ESTATE (AND YOU SHOULD NOT COUNT ON APPRECIATION WHEN DETERMINING WHETHER OR NOT TO BUY A DEAL), OVER TIME, IN THE RIGHT MARKET, THE HOUSE SHOULD APPREICATE.

DEPRECIATION
THE TAX CODE ALLOWS FOR REAL ESTATE TO BE DEPRECIATED. THIS IS A NON-CASH ITEM ON YOUR BOOKS THAT WILL LOWER YOUR TAXABLE INCOME. IF YOU ARE FULL TIME IN THE REAL ESATE BUSINESS, YOU GET A BIGGER TAX ADVANTAGE/SAVINGS. TALK TO YOUR CPA FOR FURTHER INFO.

PRINCIPAL PAY DOWN
IF YOU HAVE A LOAN ON THE PROERTY, THEN YOUR TENANT IS EFFECTIVELY MAKING YOUR PAYMENT EACH MONTH. IN DOING SO, THE PRINCIPAL AMOUNT OWED CONTINUES TO DECREASE UNTIL YOUR NOTE IS PAID IN FULL.

As I shared in my story at the beginning of this book, the first deal I decided to flip became a rental property. When I bought it, my goal was to make $20K by rehabbing it and flipping it. Unfortunately, I overestimated the ARV, underestimated the amount of work required, and of course paid way too much for it. I realized from that experience that I never again wanted to make the mistake of incorrectly evaluating a property and purchasing it too high (and you won't either after you read Section Three).

However, what I thought was a mistake at the time turned out to be very eye opening. Even with an interest rate of almost 8% on a 30-year loan, my positive cash flow initially was $430 per month (which was well in line with my cash flow goal). I just needed to target the right properties, buy them correctly, and get paid in the five different ways I mentioned.

THE IDEAL RENTAL PROPERTY

Many things make a good rental property, and I am going to cover what I believe are the most important ones to consider in this chapter. But before I discuss finding the right rental property, I want to encourage you to buy local. Stay within your city and/or metropolitan area. If you live in a rural community, I encourage you to try entering the nearest major city or suburb to buy rental properties.

Why local? It's much easier to manage in the beginning. If you have lived in your community for a while (say, two or more years), you will know the area or will at least be close enough so you can drive there if you need to do so. Managing a rental property from a distance adds a challenge you don't need in the beginning. I'm giving you this advice because I want you to have success early on. You don't want to get overwhelmed with an out-of-town rental property where you don't know what's going on and cannot effectively manage from a distance.

The bottom line is almost any house can be a rental, but some are better than others. I like to own rentals that I can sell relatively quickly if I don't want to keep it as a rental. I also like houses that have the potential to increase in value, although I

NEVER buy expecting appreciation and would NEVER use that as a reason to buy something. If you can't make a deal happen at the right price, move on to the next deal.

Finding The Right Rental Property

There are many theories about the best way to find the right rental property: reviewing the job market and local economy, school districts, crime statistics, property taxes, rental property regulations, city code enforcement, etc. All of these are important things to review before you buy a rental property in your area, and you should definitely understand them from a high level, but don't paralyze yourself with over analysis.

Another topic that may cause paralysis, but shouldn't, is evictions. I would consider it very important to know what is required to evict someone and under what circumstances before you buy your first rental property. Knowing this is going to save you time, money, and effort. If you live in an area with rent controls (like San Francisco or New York City), where it is much harder to remove a tenant from your property, it is even more important to understand these rules because you can get stuck with a problem tenant for an extended period of time.

Now that you have determined your geographic market and understand the laws regarding some worst-case scenarios, how do you narrow down your target rental property? One way is through the process of elimination. Here is a list that you can use to help you do so:

1. Vacation properties generally make bad rentals because they are not rented all the time, are cyclical depending on the economy, and are expensive to manage and maintain (i.e., you generally need to furnish them and have them cleaned regularly).

2. Condos (short for condominiums) have downside risks that eliminate them from the list. When you own a condo, you technically own the individual unit, and the common areas, along with the land, are owned collectively by all of the owners. When the market turns downward, condos are usually the first

to be affected in terms of value. When this happens, some of the condo owners stop paying their HOA dues, and when the HOA runs out of money, values drop further. I don't want to over generalize here because condos may be a good investment in your area if that is the predominate form of housing in your market; however, if they are not, don't buy them.

3. Properties in any part of town where there is higher crime, illegal drug activity, or are known as unsafe areas should be avoided. Any area you would not want to drive through day or night needs to be eliminated from your search.

4. Any property in an area where you generally cannot get sold comparable data because most of the houses sell off market should be avoided.

5. Conversely, the neighborhood that has $1M+ homes is probably off limits for your next rental.

6. If a property will not rent for 1% of the market value or better, I would pass on it. For example, if a house has a market value of $180,000 and will not rent for $1,800, move on to the next one.

7. Look at what you can afford and start there. Find a mortgage specialist that finances non-owner occupied rental properties. Fannie Mae (as of this writing) will allow you to finance up to 10 non-owner occupied properties on 30-year mortgages at the best market interest rates available. For example, if you qualify for no more than $120,000 then you should not be looking at deals where you would need to finance $150,0000.

Lower End vs. Higher End

Just because a house can be a rental property doesn't necessarily mean it can be a good rental property. Let's say homes in Middlesville, America range in value from $50,000 to

$1,000,000. I wouldn't want to rent on either end of that spectrum, meaning I wouldn't want to own a rental property worth $50,000 or $1,000,000. Why?

Lower End

At the lower end of the market you are probably in an area where the property management is going to require more involvement from you or your manager. Tenants have more issues at the lower end of the spectrum. What issues? Issues like paying their rent on time!

Generally speaking, the homes in this area tend to stay lower in value and certainly don't appreciate like homes in the median sales price/value range. One major reason is the limited financing available at the lower end of the spectrum. There are no government-backed mortgage loans available under $50,000.

So what? Well, I realize I am generalizing here, and I know every market is different, but think for a minute. If there is limited financing available, the majority of the owner occupants in this area will be smaller, and those who do own their own homes will either have to buy them for cash or buy with some type of seller financing.

The reality is a large portion of property owners in an area of town like this are landlords, and by default they will keep values lower. Why? Because there will not be enough retail sales available (most investors are buying these off market, meaning not on the MLS, and probably at a deep discount), so there will be little to no sold comparable properties. When comparable properties (sold comps) don't exist, the values become very difficult to determine and will effectively remain low. It's the reality of the market cycle in the lower end part of town.

Even though I wouldn't buy for appreciation, I certainly wouldn't want to buy knowing something isn't going to appreciate for a very long period of time, if ever. Even though lower-end homes can produce great cash flow if managed correctly, they can also be a management nightmare with the quality of tenant you are going to attract.

Higher End

On the opposite end of the spectrum, you have homes that are not attainable for the average American, let alone most real estate investors. The reality is even if you are a high net worth individual looking for rental properties, buying a rental house in the $1M range can be a challenging investment because there is a limited number of renters in this range. Even if you did have a great tenant situation, when the market does turn down and/or you lose this tenant, it's going to be very difficult for you to find a replacement. Also, if you decided to sell, how long is it going to take to move a deal like this? More than likely, it's going to take much longer than a house in the median sales price range, which will have a larger pool of buyers.

Of course, there are always exceptions, and you may have an area of town where none of this is true. Major cities like New York City and San Francisco may be exceptions, especially in a strong market. However, I would avoid any houses considered higher end for your particular market. This doesn't mean just $1M houses. It could be anything above $250,000 or something even lower than this.

What Would I Target?

Ideally, I target houses with three bedrooms, two bathrooms, a two-car garage, and less than 2,000 square feet. I also like them to have central heating and air conditioning, and be built after 1978. I would find the median (or middle) home valve, and target that as my starting point.

For example, if the median value of a home in your area is $150,000, then I would target houses with values no more than this, and make sure the rental comps are at 1% or greater. This means if the house is worth $150,000, I would want the rent to be at least $1,500 or greater. I also like rent houses where there are multiple investing strategies and that can be easily sold. This means I can wholesale it or flip it if I wanted to do so.

RENTAL FORMULA FOR SUCCESS

So what do your rental property numbers need to look like for you to consider it a deal? Great question. For rentals, you are going to need to know four things before you commit to purchasing a property:

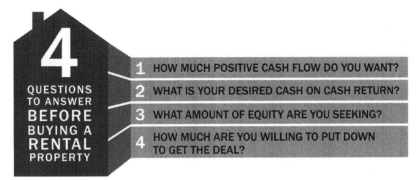

4 QUESTIONS TO ANSWER BEFORE BUYING A RENTAL PROPERTY

1 HOW MUCH POSITIVE CASH FLOW DO YOU WANT?

2 WHAT IS YOUR DESIRED CASH ON CASH RETURN?

3 WHAT AMOUNT OF EQUITY ARE YOU SEEKING?

4 HOW MUCH ARE YOU WILLING TO PUT DOWN TO GET THE DEAL?

The answers to these questions are subjective and personal. Each investor has different requirements. You will need to determine what works for you. If you haven't answered these questions, then you don't know what to look for yet. I have seen many investors waste a lot of time trying to figure out if they have a deal or not because they didn't know these answers. Let's get into some detail here to help you.

Positive Cash Flow

This is the amount of money you make each month after you pay Principal, Interest, Taxes, and Insurance (aka PITI). If you own fewer than ten properties, have good credit, low debt-to-income (DTI), and some cash reserves, you can qualify for a long-term loan (30-year mortgage) at the best interest rate on the market. Once you have a ballpark interest rate that you can use, you need to get a mortgage calculator (or use a free one online) to determine your principle and interest (P&I).

You then need to look at the property tax records (also found online for most areas), and divide that annual number by 12 to get a monthly amount.

Find an insurance agent who focuses on non-owner occupied rental properties and do the same calculation for your hazard insurance policy.

For example, say you have a $90,000 mortgage and the interest rate is 4.5% (typical as of this writing):

- P&I = $456/month
- Assume annual property taxes are $3,000 per year, which is $250/month
- An insurance approximation is around $900/year or $75/month
- This makes the total PITI $781/moth. If you can rent the house for $1,200/month you would have $419 in positive cash flow per month

The question you have to ask is this enough to buy this deal? But before you answer, let's look at the others things in our list.

Cash-on-Cash Return

Cash-on-cash return means how much I need to put down to yield the percentage return I am looking to make. In most cases, I want to put down the lowest amount possible and get the biggest return on my money. The same probably holds true for most investors.

Cash-on-cash return is calculated by taking the total positive cash flow for the year ($4,908 in the above example), and dividing it by the amount you have to bring to closing on your purchase. For example, if you have to bring $20,000 to closing to purchase the property, your cash-on-cash return would be 24.5%. Is that a good return? Hmmm...where else can you get a 24.5% return on your money? What if you have some major expense of say $2,000? That takes your cash-on-cash return to 14.5%. Still, where can you get 14.5% on your money in today's market?

Equity

The best advice I can give you is never buy a property without equity. To calculate equity, you need to take the After Repair Value (ARV) of the property and subtract your total cost (you can include your total acquisition cost if you like, but it's not necessary).

For example, you have a house with an ARV of $180,000. It needs $50,000 in work and you are going to buy it for $76,000 (a great deal by the way). Here you would have $54,000 in equity, not including any of your costs. What is the minimum amount of equity that you need to make it a deal for you? This, of course, is a personal preference. I like to have 30% equity, but you can be totally fine with 20% or 10%. Just don't purchase a deal with negative equity.

Amount You Need to Close

There is no question that this is an important number, no matter what deal you are doing, and it ultimately comes down to how much money you have available to you for investing purposes. I included this here because you may have to decide if you want to spread this amount over more than one deal based on your investing goals. If you are in a position where you don't have enough reserves to do one deal, you may need to build more capital or buy the deal low enough where you can bring a very small amount to closing to get your deal purchased with the right kind of financing. We will discuss this more in *Chapter 20: Funding Your Deals*.

PROPERTY MANAGEMENT

If you want to learn the ins and outs of the rental property business, my suggestion is manage your rental property(s) until you do your first eviction. It's inevitable at some point, so I would plan on knowing what to do when the situation occurs. This involves some research regarding the laws in your area. Get to know them before you purchase a rental property.

Most evictions are due to tenants not paying rent. Leaving someone in your property for too long without collecting rent is a really bad idea. I heard a friend of mine say, "The longer you wait to evict a tenant that isn't paying you, the cheaper you are making it for them to move." My advice is never wait to start the process.

If you are not in a position to manage any property yourself because you work too many hours, or are out of town enough to where you cannot do it effectively, then you will need to find a property manager. How do you find a good one? Once again, I would start with your local real estate investor clubs, your mastermind group (if it has been established), or even a real estate agent or broker who works with investors.

Without spending too much time on property management (as that can be an entire book by itself), here are three key things to consider when selecting one that will help you streamline the process:

1. Find one that has successfully been in the business for a long time. I would look for ten years or more. If you cannot find one in your area with this level of experience, get someone with no less than five years. The more experience the better because they will have managed in different market cycles with various tenant situations.

2. Look for one who personally owns rental property and is not just a property manager. This type of property manager will be able to relate to you as a mutual property owner and will be able to see things from your perspective.

3. Choose someone who has their own work crews and does not have to subcontract all of the maintenance and repairs. This will keep your costs to a minimum.

SECTION THREE
DUE DILIGENCE

CHAPTER 10

INTRODUCTION TO DUE DILIGENCE

So far we have covered a lot of ground, and I hope that things are clicking for you and making sense. From laying the foundation for real estate investing to investing strategies, these sections were written to provide a framework for you to get started in real estate investing. With that said, everything that we have discussed up to this point is totally irrelevant if you skip this section or merely gloss over it.

If you are skipping around in this book and starting with this chapter, you are now reading the most important material. Yes, I know finding deals is important, and that section is next. But what good is finding a deal if you don't know if it is really a deal or not? Without some due diligence you will never know what kind of deal you may be getting. Keep that in mind as we continue.

By definition *due diligence* in the real estate investing world means taking steps to evaluate a deal to determine the property's After Repair Value (ARV), as well as any necessary repairs and/or tangible improvements you are going to make to achieve the ARV. Uncovering anything unforeseen or unexpected prior to any closing should be your objective. Keep in mind, you don't have to do this all by yourself, and you should use multiple experienced resources to assist you that we are going to discuss shortly. The key is you are going to need to do some form of due diligence to ultimately protect yourself from losing money.

In real estate, there are always things that pop up, either big or small, that can bite you after you have already purchased the property. Listen to me here. It's going to happen to you no matter what. I don't care if you are a new investor or experienced or if you are buying an old or brand-new house. You will find something that doesn't work, is broken, or maybe worse. That's why it's critical to perform as much due diligence as you can on each deal prior to closing.

So what can pop up unexpectedly?

1. Plumbing issues surprise investors more than anything else, and probably cost investors the most money to repair when compared to any other item. Houses built before 1980 were primarily built using cast iron pipes for the drain lines. These have a shelf life of 40 to 50 years before they rust and/or break. When they break they start to leak under the house and can cause foundation problems. Re-piping a house is very expensive and can compromise a slab foundation if not done properly.

2. Roofing is another issue that surprises investors all the time and often goes unchecked by a professional during a walkthrough of the house. While some roofs appear to be functioning well, they could have hail damage or are close to their end of life. If you are not experienced in knowing what to look for, get someone qualified to inspect the roof before you buy the house.

3. HVAC inspections by a professional almost never occur during an assessment of a property. By professional, I mean sending someone qualified to service a unit to inspect it for proper size as well as overall function. While the system may be heating or cooling when you did your walk through of the property, that doesn't mean it will after you purchase it. When the unit stops working because the coil is

filthy, compressor freezes, or the system is at the end of its functional life, the cost can be several thousand dollars to replace.

In summary, you need to know three things to determine if you have a deal you may want to take. They are:

3 THINGS TO DETERMINE IF IT'S A DEAL YOU WANT TO TAKE

1. THE AFTER REPAIR VALUE (ARV)
2. THE NECESSARY REPAIRS AND/OR TANGIBLE IMPROVEMENTS YOU ARE MAKING
3. THE PURCHASE PRICE

In fact, you will need the first two in order to determine what purchase price you are willing to pay for the property. Before we get into this discussion, here are the definitions of the terms we will be using in this section.

SECTION THREE GLOSSARY

Appraisal: This is a report performed by a licensed real estate appraiser that provides the value of a property based on market facts, as well as subjectivity, along with how that value was determined.

Functional Obsolescence: According to the *Dictionary of Real Estate Appraisal, Fifth Edition* (Appraisal Institute), functional obsolescence is "the impairment of functional capacity of a property according to market tastes and standards." The Appraisal Institute's book, *The Appraisal of Real Estate, Thirteenth Edition*, states, "Functional obsolescence may be caused by a deficiency or a superadequacy. Some forms are curable and others are incurable."

—**Deficiency**: a type of functional obsolescence that is basically the lack of something that other properties in the subject's neighborhood have. An example would be a poor floor plan that has a bedroom that can only be accessed through another bedroom.

—**Superadequacy**: a type of functional obsolescence that exceeds what is typical for the properties in the area and does not contribute to the overall value in an amount equal to its cost (i.e., putting $30,000 worth of appliances in a house worth $90,000).

Garage Conversion: This involves transforming a functional garage (one that is typically and primarily used for automobile storage as well as storage for tools/equipment/supplies and other items not stored inside the premises) into livable space.

Real Estate Appraiser: A professionally licensed expert who assesses a property to estimate or determine the value via a documented report called an appraisal.

Sold Comparable (Sold Comp): This refers to a property that most closely resembles the property you are evaluating for purchase.

Subject Property: This refers to the specific deal that you are evaluating for purchase.

CHAPTER 11

DETERMINING THE ARV

I n real estate investing, everything starts with determining the value. By value, we mean the After Repair Value, or ARV. When you are talking to other investors about a deal you are working on, the first thing they are going to ask you is, "What is the ARV?" It doesn't matter what investing option you are implementing (i.e., wholesale, flip or rental property), you have to know the ARV.

This number refers to the value of the property after you complete all of the rehab/repairs, or what I like to call the tangible improvements to the property. The value means what the property could sell for in its specific market right now. This amount is too important to simply be left to uninformed guesswork or data that comes from online sources not directly tied to MLS sold comparable properties.

Many states are non-disclosure states, which means they do not have to provide data on sold properties to the general public. Each state has its own laws on this, and there are around a dozen or so as of this writing that are non-disclosure. In such states, the only way sales information can be obtained is from a subscription to the MLS, which only real estate agents and brokers have access to as part of their membership.

The Importance of Analyzing Sold Properties

Listing statuses vary based on where you live and the MLS being used. Let me explain some of them that are used in North Texas:

1. **Active**: The property is available for sale

2. **Pending**: The property is under contract awaiting closing

3. **Sold**: The title has been conveyed to a new owner and the property has closed and funded

4. **Expired**: The property was listed for a specific period of time that was determined by the seller and their real estate agent, and that time has now lapsed and the listing is no longer active

5. **Terminated**: The listing was terminated for some reason that is probably not disclosed

So an active listing is just that, active. It has not sold. Pending properties are not sold either, so don't use them to determine a deal you are evaluating. A property can also be pending at one price and sell at a lower or higher price.

Sold properties reflect what an actual buyer is willing to pay for a given property in a specific market, at a specific time, in its current condition. You might have an opinion after evaluating a specific property that it is worth more or less than a comparable, but remember, *it's only worth what someone is willing to pay for it.*

When determining the ARV for a single-family property, sold comparable properties (a.k.a. sold comps) are what are always evaluated first because there was a buyer that determined what they were actually willing to pay for the property.

Appraisers actually have to do different things when sold comps are not available due to market conditions. For our purposes, you need to use sold comps only. We can spend a lot more time here going through the nuances that can arise, but it's not important for what we are trying to accomplish. Once you get more experience, some of this will make more sense to you.

Active properties, for the most part, are your competition. When you are assessing the scope of work needed to improve the property, keep this in mind and be sure to look at the actives, not only for the price they are listed for but also their condition. An active comparable that is superior to and priced lower than your deal is likely going to sell before yours does.

I want to spend some time talking about all three methods you can use to determine the After Repair Value of a property.

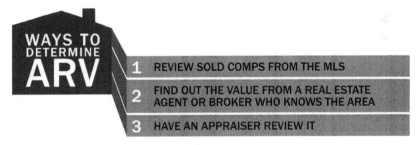

WAYS TO DETERMINE ARV

1 REVIEW SOLD COMPS FROM THE MLS

2 FIND OUT THE VALUE FROM A REAL ESTATE AGENT OR BROKER WHO KNOWS THE AREA

3 HAVE AN APPRAISER REVIEW IT

REVIEWING SOLD COMPS

This topic is absolutely critical to your success in real estate investing. If you are not a licensed real estate agent or broker, and don't have access to MLS data, you will need to see if there is a subscription-based provider of MLS data where you are located (in the Dallas/Fort Worth market, Propelio.com is one good option), or find someone who has access and can provide this for you.

With that said, if you are running comps for the first time (or first ten times), you are going to need some help from a good real estate agent, a good appraiser who knows the area well, or an experienced investor who can help you evaluate your deal.

Do not attempt to determine the ARV by yourself until you understand how to do it effectively. When it comes to reviewing sold comps on your own, you need to be sure you are looking at the right data when determining a comparable.

In order for a property to be considered comparable to the subject property, it needs to meet certain criteria. The following are some key guidelines for you to consider:

- **Try to find at least three comps**. Remember, one comp is not enough to determine the ARV. You need to find at least three in order to determine the ARV because this is how an appraiser is going to do it. There are some exceptions. Going into deeper detail now is not my intended purpose for this book.

- **Stay within the major subdivision of the subject property**. Try to find properties that are as close to the subject property as possible. Don't travel over one mile to get sold comps unless you absolutely have to do so.

- **Do not cross any major roads or highways**. Sometimes crossing a major road, intersection, or highway, etc., can give you a false impression of what the value might be as one side may have higher values than the other side for similar properties. You may not understand why until you drive the area to see. Certainly, if you cannot find any comps (or enough comps) you may have to cross over to find some.

- **Stay within the tightest timeframe that you can.** Start with comps that have sold in the last 90 days or less, and then incrementally expand your timeframe to one year if you cannot find enough data.

- **Find homes built in a similar time period**. This means homes built in the 1920s and 1930s should not be compared to homes built in the 1980s. Find homes built around the same time period when looking for comparables.

- **Find homes with similar square footage**. Plus or minus around 15% can be a good rule of thumb to follow to find enough data to utilize. So if the subject is 1500 square feet, select a range that goes from 1325 square feet to 1725 square feet.

- **Look for similar style homes and/or a similar builder**. Tract neighborhoods are much easier to evaluate than an area with custom built homes because many of the homes were built around the same time with very similar floor plans. You can have neighborhoods that have a mix of both. There are subdivisions and neighborhoods that have a combination of everything–older custom homes, newer custom homes, older tract homes, and newer tract homes. Be sure you are comparing the right ones when doing your evaluation!

- **Look for similar school districts**. There are subdivisions that can cross school districts that are right next to one another with similar homes to the subject. However, one area sells much higher/lower than the other, and you cannot figure out why. Be sure to look at the school district because it can have a major impact in determining value.

- **Don't just pick the highest sold comp(s)**. Many new investors like to go straight to the highest sold comp, and use that to determine the value. Look for comps that are in similar condition as the subject is going to be once completed. When an appraiser is doing an appraisal like this, it is called a "subject to" appraisal, which means the value is subject to the underlying improvements that are listed in the actual appraisal document. Also, it takes at least three comps to determine the value and not just one (and certainly not the highest one).

- **Look for any external influences**. This includes things like is the property on a busy street, does it back up to commercial property, are there high tension power lines above the house, does it back to railroad tracks, is it across the street from a school, does it side to a four-lane through street? Any of these things can have a negative impact on the value. Of course, do not neglect any influences that can have a positive impact on the value such as backing to a golf course, a wooded lot, lake view, or nature preserve.

- **Look for any functional obsolescence**. This is something that you must take into consideration, and whether it is curable or incurable.

- **Subtract any seller concessions if they exist**. Seller concessions are only found on the MLS.

That's a lot of stuff! Yes, and it's important so be sure to review it again.

So now what? Once you have all of the data, take the three best comps you have, and start comparing them to the subject a bit more. Keep narrowing it down based on the data above until you can determine what you think the ARV is. For example, if you have three sold comps that are $145,000, $150,000, and $147,000, the value is probably going to be somewhere between $145,000 and $150,000. So if you go with $147,500 you are probably going to be extremely close to the ARV.

An Example: The WRONG Way to Do It

One thing that confuses new and seasoned investors is taking the price-per-square-foot approach to determining the value (which we will address again in the next chapter). What does this mean? Let's take a look at the following comps and analyze them:

- House #1 has 1500 square feet and sold for $145,000 or $96.67/square foot

- House #2 has 1800 square feet and sold for $150,000 or $83.33/square foot

- House #3 has 1600 square feet and sold for $147,000 or $91.88/square foot

- Subject property has 2200 square feet so the ARV should be $199,381, correct?

NO! This is incorrect!

How did this happen? This happened because the investor took the selling price and divided it by the gross living area.

So in this example, they took the three price-per-square-foot values above and added them together to get $271.88. Then they divided that number by three to get $90.63, which is the average price-per-square-foot of the three comps. When you multiply $90.63 times 2200 you get $199,381. Logically this seems to make sense; however, this is one of the biggest mistakes you can make, and sadly, it happens all the time.

The reason you DO NOT want to do this is the methodology is flawed. According to Ohio appraiser Mike Armentrout who wrote an article titled "The Reality of Price Per Square Foot":

> "The primary fault with $/SF is that it encompasses every feature of the property and not just gross living area. Only calculating the relationship between size and sales price ignores all the considerations a potential buyer may make. If we were comparing two properties that were identical with the exception of size, then it is rational that the larger of the two may sell for more and thus the $/SF could be an accurate indicator. On the other hand, if we had two identical homes in terms of size but one had a larger wooded lot and sold for more, the equation would not be as reliable. As properties have more dissimilar amenities and features, the less reliable it becomes as a function of indicating value. This is simply because other factors are not directly related to gross living area."

I couldn't agree more with this quote.

Also, given a specific market, higher square footage homes generally sell for a lower $/sqft and lower square footage homes sell for a higher $/sqft. Ask yourself the following question: would you pay 33% more (or $50,000 more in the above example) to get 400 additional square feet of living space? No, you would not. Neither would a market buyer. In fact, if there were a buyer like this for some crazy reason, the property would not appraise as the buyer might expect because there is probably no justification for a value this high.

Another flawed approach to determining value that I see ALL the time are investors taking the highest comp and using that as the value. The idea here is that if one property sold at that price then the subject property has the potential to be worth as much as well. While this may seem to make sense, one sold comp does not, in most cases, make a value. There are exceptions to everything, but try to find at least three sold comps as stated at the beginning of this section to determine value.

Sometimes the ARV will be very obvious and right in line with what you, an agent, or appraiser would expect if they were doing a desktop review (looking at sold comps on the MLS online). Other times, it will be very challenging depending on the data you have at your disposal. As I mentioned above, you absolutely want someone to help you with this while you are getting started because determining the ARV correctly is critical.

Don't get overwhelmed. Once you do it over and over again, you will get the hang of it. However, many investor deals are quirky (which is why they are investor deals), and could have some issues that are beyond the scope of what I just addressed. If this happens when you are going through your evaluation, and you are struggling to determine the value, you will want to enlist a real estate agent or appraiser to help you.

USING A REAL ESTATE AGENT OR BROKER

Remember in the last section how I told you that you should use a real estate agent when flipping a house? Another reason why you should build that relationship is they can help you determine your ARV. However, like I said earlier, only if they meet the criteria for a good real estate agent I mentioned in Chapter 8.

Having a good real estate agent(s) on your team is something you will build over time. It takes time because, like with any new venture, people need to see that you can perform and do what you say you are going to do (in this case we mean close on deals!), and not just be a time sucker asking them for favors.

Once an agent sees that you will close (or have closed on a deal) that gives them confidence in doing more deals with you, and they will want to help you with running comps and determining the ARV.

Make sure your agent knows the area. Nobody, not even an appraiser, has more knowledge than an agent who is actively working full time in your subject's area. In fact, a good agent who genuinely works and knows the area will have so much valuable information that appraisers often call upon them for up-to-date and in-the-know information on the current state of a particular market/submarket or about a specific deal.

How do you know if the agent you are talking to knows the area? You can see their listings and the concentration of their listings by driving the neighborhood. If you drive through the subject property's neighborhood and see more than one sign for them, that would be a good start toward selecting the right one. You can also call any broker sign you see in the neighborhood and ask which agent(s) really know this particular area.

As I stated, it's going to take time. Calling an agent and asking them to run some comps for you is probably not going to get you the results you want. Once you let them either sell a property for you or represent you on the buying side of a deal, they will probably be more than willing to help you with any values you need. In the meantime, don't be afraid to pay for an appraisal if you have the time to do so.

GETTING AN APPRAISAL

In my opinion, there is no substitute for a "boots on the ground" appraisal by an experienced appraiser who is familiar with the subject area and appraises property there on a regular basis. Why? It eliminates the guesswork in determining the value. In addition to providing you with the value of your property (either AS-IS or ARV), it will show you photos of the comps, location of the comps, and how the appraiser arrived at the value. By request, you can have the rent comps added by the appraiser as well if this is going to be a rental property, which will show the active properties for lease as well as the properties that have been leased in a certain timeframe.

The downside is appraisals can take time to get, especially if you are using a really good appraiser because they are going to be in high demand. If you are in a competitive situation, need to close quickly (like a week or less), and your appraiser is booked two weeks out, you are not going to be able to use them. Also, if you are getting financing for this purchase, you will not get to pick your appraiser; your lender will.

In this situation, you will have to rely on a real estate agent or someone else to help you. If there is too much at risk with a specific deal, you may need to get additional time from the seller or move on to the next deal. That's why it's a good idea to have a couple of good appraisers you can use.

Three Key Things a Good Appraiser Does:

1. Determines Actual Square Footage

Recently one of my hard-money clients purchased a property where the online county tax roll records said the house was 1800 square feet. When our appraiser measured it, the actual square footage was 1350 square feet, which, as you might imagine, had a tremendous negative impact on the value. The good news is my client was able to renegotiate the purchase price and get it lowered to offset the difference. But if they hadn't had it measured, they would have overpaid and most likely lost money in the deal!

For some reason many investors don't care about measuring a house to determine its actual square footage, and this is a big mistake. In Texas, most of the county appraisal districts list the square footage of each property on their website, so investors look up the property online and use that data as the truth. Unfortunately, over 25% of tax records are wrong on the square footage (some very slightly and some more severely). Many investors rely on this data too much and end up getting burned.

The first thing an appraiser does when they get to the property is measure it. Anytime you are seriously considering a house to buy, why not hire an appraiser to at least measure and comp it before you close? It's most likely cheaper than doing an actual appraisal and can save you in the long run. In fact, even if it's the same price as doing an actual appraisal, it's the cost of doing business ($500 for an appraisal versus losing $15,000 due to a mistake).

Over time and with experience, you'll begin to be able to tell the difference between a house that is 1800 square feet and one that is 1350 square feet just by looking at it or being inside it. When you get to this level (and depending on the deal you are doing), you will want to at least get an appraiser to comp it for you. Of course, it takes time for you to build a relationship and get this data.

Do not think that I am suggesting you call an appraiser to run comps for you on your first deal. I can tell you right now that they are not going to do it. However, if you hire them to do an evaluation (meaning you order an appraisal from them and pay them to do it), over time, they might help you with some comps.

2. Drives by the Sold Comps and Analyzes the Competition

Appraisers will normally drive by the sold comps they are using for the appraisal to see how they physically compare to the subject. Looking online is the starting point. After that, seeing how the property looks in person can take on a whole new meaning. Things like layout of the lot, location on the street, property amenities not seen or discoverable online can all be taken into consideration.

If you are going to be flipping the property, you may want your appraiser to help you analyze the competition (those are the active properties on the market right now) both now and when you get ready to sell the property. Why do this? It's good to know how many actives versus sold properties there are. This ratio tells you the health of that particular market.

For example, if there are five actives and one sold in the last six months, that probably indicates the market is not very strong in your area, so you may want to skip this as a flip. If the numbers are reversed and there are five sold properties and one active, that market is probably very strong and you should not have any issue selling it.

3. Looks for Obsolescence and External Influences

The glossary in this section covers what obsolescence is. If you haven't read it, I encourage you to do so. Whether it's a superadequacy or deficiency, it needs to be noted in the appraisal, and you need to be alerted to it. Things like not enough bathrooms for the number of bedrooms in a house can create functional obsolescence that otherwise might not be seen or understood by a new investor. External influences such as the property backing up to a power transformer, commercial/industrial property, drainage ditch, or other negative influence can impact the value significantly. If you have sold comps that also back to commercial property or a similar influence, the appraisal will reflect this more accurately.

So reach out to your network and find an appraiser who can help you with this. Someone in the investor community is going to know one they can recommend, and I would start there. Once you have your mastermind group going, that can be another resource for you to use in order to find the right appraiser. Many investors skip this step altogether, and from the value they deliver that I just described, you can see how it can be a big mistake not using one.

CHAPTER 12

HOW TO DETERMINE THE ARV WITH A GARAGE CONVERSION

Over the years, I have bought, sold, rented, and funded many houses with garage conversions. So, how does a garage conversion affect the value of a property? Great question, and one that confuses new and seasoned investors alike. That's why I wanted to spend a whole chapter on this.

THE CHALLENGE: NOT ALL CONVERSIONS ARE CREATED EQUAL

Garage conversions can be complicated to evaluate. Some may appear to be seamless parts of the original home, while others will give the appearance of an obvious conversion, because it looks and functions differently from the rest of the house.

What many investors fail to realize is that in any conversion, functional parking and storage space are lost. So any potential "gain" has to be weighed against the value lost to the garage/patio/other space. To properly evaluate any such conversion, the buyer must first ask a series of basic questions:

1. Is the newly created space necessary, or is it simply creating an over-improvement?

2. Is the functional use of the home better, or worse off, with this conversion?

3. What is the quality and functionality of the finished product?

4. Was the conversion permitted by the city?

To answer the first two questions, look at the broader market. Many investors feel like anytime additional living area can be added, it will guaranty a return, but this is not always the case.

For example, in a community of 3 bedroom/1 bath and 3 bedroom/2 bath homes, is it really necessary to have a 5 bedroom,/1 bath home? In that same community, would a second, or even third living area be well received? Probably not, especially if it means surrendering, and thus losing, the value of enclosed parking or valuable storage in a neighborhood in which the primary occupant may be blue collar workers with trade tools to store.

Often, the easiest way to determine market demand for this sort of "improvement" may be to simply stand in front of the home and note if any other homes in the area have similar conversions. If none are noted, then it is likely a good indication of a lack of market demand. Remember, every micro market is different.

Once you have determined market demand for a conversion, then you can evaluate its financial return in the market. Keep in mind that you have lost parking and storage, so you will be starting at a deficit. Thus, any monetary return must exceed the financial loss from the parking before it makes sense.

Whew! That can be a bit much to grasp, but this is exactly what an appraiser is going to do when evaluating a house like this.

With this in mind, there are two basic types of conversions you will encounter: the Do-It-Yourselfer and the Professional Conversion.

TYPES OF CONVERSIONS

The Do-It-Yourselfer

This is typically the most common type of conversion you will encounter. If the house you are evaluating has this type of conversion, it will more than likely not add any value and could very well even reduce the value after considering the loss of parking. These conversions are easily recognizable because they typically:

- Have a noticeable step down and/or sloped floors
- Have dis-functional access and an odd shape or oversized room (a 20' by 20' room with few or no windows).
- Have little or no wall and attic insulation
- Can have undersized cooling and heating systems or even separate window units.

The best approach when encountering this sort of conversion, in absence of consulting with an appraiser, is to attribute it a zero-value return, as any gain will likely be offset by the loss of parking.

Professional Conversions

On the other hand, I have seen some garage conversions that were so professionally done, you could not tell the house ever had a garage. If the conversion is professionally and correctly done, it will typically look seamless to the rest of the house:

- Same level flooring (no slope and no step to get to the next room),
- A vent drop for a common HVAC with the appropriate amount of tonnage (i.e., no window unit supporting the space)
- Appropriate siding in place of the overhead garage door.
- Free from any functional obsolescence

- Of comparable finish to the rest of the home.

- Most importantly, the new space enhances the functionality and use of the home, relative to the neighborhood while remaining within a reasonable size range.

For example, a 2 bedroom/1 bath home in a neighborhood that contains many, if not mostly, 3 bedroom/2 bath homes, would likely do well to have a garage conversion to transform the home into a functional, seamless, 3/2 design, particularly if the existing garage is a smallish sized, single car garage, which would not likely be utilized for parking modern sized cars.

Another note: it's good to determine whether the conversion was properly permitted by the city. In some cases, certain long-term lenders will not allow the appraiser to count the additional square footage if it was not properly permitted.

DETERMINING THE VALUE

When it comes to determining the value of a home with a garage conversion, there are two ways to go about it: the right way, and the wrong way. I know that sounds obvious, but I have a point. Let's talk about each to be sure you are clear on the differences:

The Incorrect Approach

We discussed this in the previous chapter, but it's important to cover it again with a specific scenario so you do not make this mistake when doing an evaluation. When evaluating a house with a garage conversion, I typically see the following investor approach, one that I like to call, flat out wrong:

The investor will add the square footage of the conversion to the overall livable square footage of the house, and then look at price per square foot of sold properties (many times using comps without garage conversions) to determine the value of the subject property. This approach is what gets investors into trouble....

Let's consider the following as an example. You have a house in a given area that has 3 bedrooms, 2 baths with 1400 sqft plus a 400 sqft garage. The garage gets converted to a living room, so you add that square footage to the overall number making it 1800 sqft. However, the homes in the area range from 1100-1500 sqft with a similar bed/bath count and two-car garages.

Additionally, the homes in the area sell for $100 per square foot, putting the top value at $150,000 of any sold comp. You take the $100 per square foot and multiply that times 1800, giving the subject property a value of $180,000 or 20% higher than the highest comp. Do you think you calculated the correct market value?

What you must do is ask yourself, if you were an occupant buyer, would you pay 20% more for a house in a given area to get 400 square feet more living space and not have a functional garage? The answer to that is probably not.

In fact, the property will more than likely not appraise for a value this high for the same reason. *What many investors forget to do is put themselves in the position of an occupant buyer when evaluating a property's value.*

The Correct Way to Determine Value

Here is the correct approach to evaluating a property with a converted garage: if there are supporting comps with converted garages, use as many of those as you can to evaluate the subject property. However, if you cannot find any supporting comps, then you have to back out the garage (by subtracting the additional square footage), and evaluate the property with the comps available to determine the value. Why? Because:

1. The square footage of a garage is not included in the overall square footage of the house because it's not considered livable space.

2. A conversion, even if professionally and correctly done, could add square footage to a house making it larger than any of the area comps without conversions, potentially forcing larger adjustments to be made to determine the value.

When evaluating a property with a garage conversion, three results can occur: its value will (1) increase, (2) remain the same, or (3) decrease. Which of the three it does is based on what the market is telling you in that area. This can also change as market conditions change.

In some cases, not having a garage (even with a nice conversion) can actually lower the value of the property. We have seen this many times, and it bothers investors because they cannot understand why that additional square footage does not help. You have to put yourself in the shoes of an occupant buyer to understand. Such a buyer (especially true in properties with higher values) most likely wants a garage to park their cars and store things. If that's not available, they will find another house that offers this.

Of course, this is not always the case, since there are no absolutes in real estate. However, you don't have to guess at whether this is the case or not because the appropriate comps are the evidence that support the correct value. Use those comps, and you should be able to determine the market value of a house with a converted garage.

CHAPTER 13

DETERMINING THE NECESSARY TANGIBLE IMPROVEMENTS AND SCOPE OF WORK

Determining the value of a property is just one part of your due diligence as you evaluate a potential deal. Equally important is determining the tangible improvements to the property that will be required in order to achieve the correct ARV along with their line item and grand total cost. It's not just the necessary repairs that are needed, but the items required to improve the value of a property to reach the ARV.

WHY THIS IS SO IMPORTANT

You must, as accurately as possible, determine each line item that needs to be addressed in the scope of work so you will be able to make the most effective offer you can that will allow you to make the assignment fee you desire, the profit amount you are seeking if you are flipping, or the returns you must have to keep this deal as a rental. Without an accurate scope of work, you may end up offering too much or too little, and either lose money or lose the deal. It's not only important that you make money, but you never want to lose any money!

BEING A REAL ESTATE INVESTOR VS. A GENERAL CONTRACTOR

Let me start by expressing that even if you are a contractor or a very handy person and can do a lot of the labor yourself, I don't want you to focus on doing any of the work yourself. It's fine to create the scope of work, and I encourage you to do this as you have that as an area of expertise. When it comes to lifting a hammer or a paintbrush, don't do it! Of course you can do what you want, but it's important that I state this so you can at least have it in the back of your mind for every deal you are evaluating.

If you are in real estate investing to work on houses, then you are defeating the purpose of being a real estate investor. Every time you lift a hammer or a paintbrush, you transfer from being an investor to being a contractor. I can hear some readers saying, "Well, I can do this myself and save thousands." Really? How much is your time worth? Wouldn't it be worth more for you to spend that time looking for your next deal? Are you an investor or a contractor? If you are reading this book, I hope you say investor and leave the work to qualified contractors.

To identify a good general contractor, refer to that section in Chapter 8.

HOW TO DETERMINE THE SCOPE OF WORK (SOW)

The easiest and most effective way to determine the scope of work (especially when you are new) is to have a general contractor(s) give you an estimate, but be there each time they do the walk through so you can understand what is going on and learn from the experience. Your initial goal should be to walk into a house and assess in $5,000 increments what the cost will be to complete the project. Over time, and with more experience, you will be able to walk into any house and know the cost and the overall scope within 10% of the actual number. Costs for work vary based on where you are located and the price of labor and materials in your market. Here are the steps you can take to determine the scope of work for each deal you are evaluating:

Step 1: Get access to the property: Whether the deal is on the MLS or from an individual seller, you will need to get access to the property by getting an appointment to see it. Make sure your contractor is available to meet you there at the same time. The goal here is for them to provide you with a complete scope of work with the associated costs for each major item.

Step 2: Take photos or video: Over the past several years, smart phones have become ideal for taking photos and video with superior quality good enough to document a property. Please use your smart phone for this purpose. This sounds easy, but in reality, getting photos or video taken requires a bit of planning and being prepared at the proper time. This is because in a situation where the seller is highly motivated to sell, you may only get one chance to go inside the house, and you are on their schedule. I would make sure your phone is charged and has enough storage to capture the amount of photos and videos you are going to take.

Make that appointment count by documenting as much as you can of the entire property, but there's no need for 100 photos because that can be confusing.

It's amazing what you will forget about a house after you leave. If you do not take photos or a video of it, you are sure to miss something. When you look back over the photos later, you may also discover things you did not realize were there. So make sure you don't take too many photos but get what you need. Make sure to always take the following photos:

- Front of the house, both sides, rear of the house and backyard.
- Any trees outside and/or plants. Trees growing adjacent to the house to where they are almost touching can cause serious damage to the foundation and/or roof. Anything growing over the roofline will need

to be trimmed away from it. Branches from trees typically follow the root system. This means that if you have branches over the roofline there are probably roots underneath this portion of the foundation, which can impact the integrity of the foundation.

- Take an inside photo of each room from the corner of the room to get the most viewing area.

- Take a photo of the hot water heater (along with the install date if it's on the sticker), electrical panel, and HVAC unit (inside and out) along with the serial number label, to verify the correct size with your contractor.

- Take photos of the bathrooms, shower/tub, fixtures, vanities, etc.

- In the kitchen, be sure to take a photo of the countertops, cabinets, and under the kitchen sink.

- Anything else that pops out that has the potential to be an issue that will need to be addressed (i.e., an above ground hot tub, evidence of termites, etc.).

Technology makes it easy. There is no excuse for not doing this at every property you are evaluating. Memorize this list, and make taking these photos a habit.

Step 3: Use your SOW spreadsheet: Use the SOW spreadsheet included in the appendix of this book (Item 2.C) as a checklist, or use a smart phone app that can help you as you do a walk through of the property. Focus on major items first, or what we like to call The Big Five:

1. **Roofing:** If you are not qualified to analyze a roof to see if it has hail damage or is at the end of its natural life, you will need to get someone qualified to determine this for you. Roof replacement can be a significant cost that should not be overlooked because it will absolutely come up during an inspection. New roofing would encompass replacing an entire roof as

opposed to including the detailed items that go with roofing, such as any decking, flashing, drip edge, etc. Conversely, roof repair would be its own line item with a cost associated with it for the necessary repairs. Determine the cost for these items along with the labor to install from your contractor.

2. **Foundation Repair:** If a house has settlement beyond acceptable norms, it may need piers to stabilize the foundation. Exterior piers are generally placed along the grade beam six feet apart, depending on the elevations around the perimeter of the house. Interior piers may be required as well. I always get my foundation company to tell me the number of piers required for a slab foundation and/or any adjustments or piers required for a pier and beam foundation. The cost for this is typically based on the number of piers needing to be installed. On a pier and beam foundation, the cost can also be based on any beams that need to be replaced due to failure, wood rot, etc.

3. **Plumbing:** This can overwhelm investors more than any other repair to a house because it's not necessarily visible during a walkthrough and often goes unseen. If you are doing any foundation work where a slab is being adjusted, it's important to get a plumbing test to make sure the drain lines are intact and their integrity has not been compromised. Houses built before 1980 typically have cast iron pipes. As mentioned previously, these can deteriorate with age. A slab leak over time can cause serious foundation problems. When the drain lines have to be replaced in a house with a slab foundation, the cost can be very expensive (like $5,000 for a complete re-pipe). Even houses with pier and beam foundations can be expensive to re-pipe, although not as much as a slab because there is a crawl space to access under the house. Check with your contractor to determine the cost in your area.

4. **HVAC:** Many factors go into determining the size of an HVAC system, so I will call my HVAC contractor to get a quote based on certain parameters. For a complete system not including the ductwork, the cost is going to be mostly based on the tonnage required to regulate the interior temperature of the house.

5. **Electrical:** Generally, the electrical work that gets most investors is an unsafe panel and/or aluminum wiring. Panels made by Federal Pacific, Zinsco, and others, are known fire hazards, and in some cases need to be replaced. I have seen the cost be anywhere from $800 to $1,500 depending on labor and materials required. Many houses built during the Vietnam War era had aluminum wiring due to a copper shortage. Aluminum wiring can expand and contract causing fires at the outlet. I know this from personal experience! However, it can be fixed through a process called "pigtailing," which your electrician will know how to do. I paid about $1,200 to pigtail an 1800 square foot rental house.

Step 4: Determining your finish out: The next step in determining the cost and scope of the work is deciding, based on comps in the area, what tangible improvements you are going to make to maximize the ARV. This involves not only looking at the sold comps, but also the actives, which are basically your competition. If the subject's comps have upgrades like hardwood flooring, stainless steel appliances, and granite countertops, you are going to need similar materials if you are going to be competitive and get your property sold.

Depending on your investing strategy (i.e., wholesale, flip, or rental), your overall scope of work may need to be adjusted. If you are wholesaling a deal, you may want to adjust the scope depending on what you think the investing strategy is going to be for your buyer. If you are flipping, you may need to adjust up to include any upgrades that may be needed.

To quickly get to a number for estimating purposes, try to do this with a price-per-square-foot approach for general cosmetics (interior and exterior paint, basic flooring, fans, fixtures, etc.), and then add any necessary upgrades mentioned.

For example, if you have a 2000 square foot house and determine from your contractor that $15 per foot will cover the general cosmetics, that cost is going to be $30,000. If you have to upgrade the countertops to granite for $2,500, and install hardwood flooring for $6,000, you need to add $8,500 in upgrades totaling $38,500. Finally, add any of The Big Five discussed, and you will have your grand total.

USING OTHER RESOURCES (Contractors and Inspectors)

Contractors

Some words of caution and advice: we have all heard horror stories about bad contractors, and I have already talked about this at length. Still, it bears repeating: Reputation is key with any contractor. If you are just looking for the cheapest one you can find, you are more than likely going to get cheap results.

As I mentioned previously, you need a primary and AT LEAST two backup contractors. Your GC should also have a primary and two backups for each tradesman/sub (i.e., a primary electrician and two backup electricians if one is not available or does not work out). Make sure the backups are just as reliable as the primary contractors we discussed previously. Also, take your contractor with you so they can help you determine your scope of work, at least until you are comfortable understanding how to do this yourself.

Inspectors

In some instances, but certainly not all, it may make sense to get a home inspection. Home inspectors will find things that your contractor will certainly overlook. Why? It's what they are trained to do. Getting an inspection from a licensed inspector is not going to give you a scope of work, but will point out some red flags that you may need to address.

Nothing scares buyers more than a home inspection because they find things that most people are not going to discover. The older the home, the more issues it can potentially have, particularly as it relates to current property code (i.e., energy efficient windows, proper insulation, electrical and plumbing codes, even down to address numbers properly displayed on the back of the house).

Time is the biggest factor in getting an inspection, especially if you are in a competitive situation with other investors ready to pay cash, close in a week, and are willing to forego an inspection. Also, sellers may not want to allow an inspection because anything you tell them about the property will more than likely need to be disclosed to the next buyer, and of course they don't want you to have any more ammo to hit them with in terms of negotiating a better price.

While an inspection can highlight a lot of problems with a house, it can also alert you to what your buyer is going to see when they inspect it upon a sales contract. Better to know this now and build it into your scope of work prior to making your offer. In many cases, the market will dictate whether you get an inspection or not. Hotter markets with buyers ready to go will eliminate you getting an inspection if you want the deal, while depressed markets can make inspections a tool to use to help drive the price down and alert you to any less obvious issues.

An inspection is limited in terms of its scope and is designed to point out things that are visible. A licensed inspector (in most cases) is not an engineer. They may see evidence of settling, but they aren't going to tell you in the report to install X number of piers to stabilize the foundation. They will have language in the report that says either the foundation is performing or not performing as intended.

This can be confusing at times since inspections are filled with disclaimers to limit the liability of the inspector. You sometimes wonder what in the world you are looking at in the inspection report, but after looking at several of them, you will be able to quickly identify which items are going to present issues you will need to get addressed.

An inspection report will also point out items that your buyer will end up seeing in their inspection report that you can have addressed ahead of time. For example, if the HVAC has a drip pan that is corroded or rusted with holes in it, that will be noted in the inspection report. If the hot water heater isn't elevated to a certain height required by code, that would be noted as well. The point here is to use these reports to your advantage to prepare for future code inspections and sales.

SUMMARY

Remember, this entire process of determining the overall scope of work will get easier with each deal you evaluate. Once you have the costs down, you will be able to make an offer that will give you confidence. You will also experience losing deals to others who will not do this correctly and will absolutely pay too much for a property. Don't be that investor who pays too much!

One last note before moving on, once you start a project, I highly encourage you to visit the site and speak with your contractor on a regular basis to (1) make sure work is going on as planned and (2) get an understanding of what you are paying for as the project progresses.

Easier Than You Think

SECTION FOUR
DEALS

CHAPTER 14

FINDING DEALS

We are now going to discuss the portion of the book that you have been waiting for since the beginning. You may want to review the other sections again after you read this because it will help solidify the entire theme of this book. At the end of the day, everything comes down to deals—finding them and transacting them.

Ultimately, everything in real estate starts with finding deals. In my professional career, I have spent far more time answering questions, speaking to groups, and spending one-on-one time consulting with clients about finding deals than almost everything else. And during that time, I've been pleased to watch the advice I have given deliver the results people are looking for in real estate investing.

I say this because I want you to know that I believe in the advice I'm giving you here 100%. I live by it, and I give it to all of my clients. My method is tested and proven to work. These aren't just ideas or half-baked theories. This is knowledge based upon actual results from my method being used in the real world. If none of this is true, I wouldn't waste your time or mine.

That being said, I want to be up front about the fact that finding deals can be challenging, and there are a number of different ways to go about it. Since there is a lot of information on ways to find deals, I want to cover what I consider the top three ways. This is based upon my personal experience, what my mastermind group does, as well as what my clients are doing.

Are there other ways to find deals beyond what I am going to discuss? Sure! But I want to cover the ones that will work in the current market. With the Internet and other evolving technology, everything is going to keep changing. There will be other ways to find deals as time progresses. But for now, let's stay focused on what I believe will work for you at this moment.

WHERE CAN YOU FIND DEALS?

Real estate investor deals can come from many places, but I want to narrow it down to what I believe are the most effective. They are:

SECTION FOUR GLOSSARY

"AS IS": Means the property is in its current condition, no matter what that condition is.

Draws: Is a monetary amount used to fund any work being performed on a property. For example, you have a loan on a property with the repair portion being held by your lender until the work is complete. Once you complete some (or all) of the work (depending on your agreement with your lender) you can request that the funds be reimbursed to you. This is done in the form of a draw request.

Equity: The difference between the ARV and total acquisition cost of the property, which may or may not include your closing costs depending on how you calculate it.

Foreclosure Listings: In Texas, properties on a foreclosure list are those that are posted at the courthouse steps 21 days prior to the auction where they are scheduled for foreclosure. This varies by state, so check what the process is in your state.

HUD: This is an acronym for the Department of Housing and Urban Development.

Pocket Buyer: This means a reliable investor that can be called directly to purchase a property from a seller (typically a wholesaler).

Probate Listings: Probate is the legal process for proving that a will is valid through a court of law that occurs after a person has died. As part of the process, an inventory of assets, including property that was owned by the deceased, is published along with their liabilities. Probate laws differ based on the state you are in, so check with your legal counsel on how to get this information if you wish to pursue this in your state.

REOs: Real Estate Owned by the bank. This is just the technical term for describing property foreclosed by a bank.

CHAPTER 15

THE MLS AND WHOLESALERS

The first way to find deals I want to discuss is the MLS (Multiple Listing Service) because it encompasses the broadest amount of real estate available for sale.

THE MLS

As explained in Section Two, the MLS is where houses get listed for sale and can be in any condition (i.e., nicely remodeled to handyman special and everything in between). This of course fluctuates with the market. For example, in a market where there are many foreclosures (e.g. 2009 – 2012) there were a lot more "deals" available on the MLS. However, as the market improved, those properties were absorbed and there were fewer and fewer "deals" available.

Keep in mind, markets are dynamic in nature. So if you don't see any deals worth buying on the MLS today, keep checking because you eventually will.

How an MLS Is Organized

MLS databases are typically organized by region and separately operated by their own private group. For example, in North Texas there is NTREIS (North Texas Real Estate Information System), which covers the Dallas/Fort Worth area, the northern section of Texas up to the Oklahoma border, as well as some of the eastern part of Texas. It is operated by an organization called MetroTex Association of REALTORS. In San Antonio there is SABOR (San Antonio Board of Realtors), which covers the San Antonio metro area as well as other portions of South Texas.

Who Can Use the MLS?

Use of the MLS is restricted to licensed professionals, such as agents, Realtors® and brokers. If you want to list your property for sale on the MLS, then you will need to have representation from one of these professionals (i.e., hire an agent) to get the property in the MLS system for all to see. This means you cannot (as of today) list your house FSBO (For Sale By Owner) on the MLS.

Information regarding sold properties is proprietary and only available for licensed professionals subscribing to the MLS service. This means you cannot directly get sold comps without access to an MLS. You can get limited access to sold comps (currently in North Texas) through a subscription service like Propelio.

MLS Style Websites and Service Platforms

Many real estate brokerages provide access to listings (i.e., active property for sale, and not sold data) on their own websites. So, if you are looking for properties for sale on the MLS, you might be able to set up a search on a broker site in your area without having to hire an agent to create alerts for you. In the beginning, this might be a good approach for you to take to familiarize yourself with how the MLS works before you get with an agent.

Other platforms that have become popular over the past several years are Zillow.com, Trulia.com and Redfin.com, which receive active listing data only through a specific format from brokers around the country every day. These active listings can be searched through their platform.

If you live in a non-disclosure state, even though these sites sometimes provide an evaluation and/or estimate of what a property is worth, it is NOT something you can rely on to determine an ARV because it is not based on sold data. I have seen this get investors into trouble many times. They use these inaccurate evaluations to determine the ARV, get a property under contract, and find out it is worth much less.

One caveat: I've read on these sites that in disclosure states, they do provide sold data. Since I work out of Texas, a non-disclosure state, I have no personal experience using such sites to find sold data, so I want to caution you to make sure you are actually getting sold data even if you are in a disclosure state where such sites could, in theory, provide it.

The majority of properties for sale in a given market are more than likely listed by licensed brokers on their respective MLS. Sellers of property are under a listing agreement with the broker allowing them to disseminate information about the property that other brokers and users of the system can access. Listings on the MLS typically include (but are not limited to) the property address, a description of the property, number of bedrooms, baths, square footage, year built, school district, days on market, listing broker contact information, etc.

Because they are listed on the open market, there will be more market exposure and potentially more competition for a given property. When there is more competition, you will generally pay a higher price for something, and this holds true for deals listed on the MLS. So, its status as an open market for buyers to make offers creates greater competition, potentially driving up prices. The types of deals on the MLS include, but are not limited to:

1. **Retail listings:** This includes any property in retail condition, ready for move in—typically targeted towards owner occupants. Retail means full price with no equity. Some, but certainly not all of the retail properties listed, will be clean, move-in ready, and even nicely remodeled. No matter what deal you are

evaluating, it must have equity or do not buy it. In my opinion, if it does not have equity it's not a deal. Therefore, retail listings should be off the table and not considered investment properties.

2. **Foreclosures** (a.k.a. REOs which means Real Estate Owned by a lender from a foreclosure sale): This includes any/all foreclosures including those from HUD. Foreclosed properties will potentially have more equity than houses listed for retail as you can probably understand. Although not always, these are basically houses that are distressed and can be purchased below market value. The question here is how much below market value and with how much equity? Foreclosures can vary in terms of price and the amount of work they require.

3. **AS-IS listings:** I would categorize these as listings that would include distressed property and/or distressed sellers. These listings may say "sold AS-IS" meaning sold in their current condition (which is probably distressed) where the seller is not willing to make any repairs to the property. Once again, these are properties that have the potential to have equity in them after they are rehabbed/repaired. However, not every AS-IS property is physically distressed. Some may be in decent condition but the seller is distressed (i.e., going through divorce, medical issues, lost their job, etc.).

I have purchased many properties on the MLS that were REOs, including HUD deals, as well as distressed houses listed for sale. As markets change (either up or down), opportunities can vary greatly on the MLS. In a hot market where everything is moving quickly, you are probably not going to find a good foreclosure deal to buy because there will be a lot of competition for it (depending on demand in your market). In a slow or downward trending market, you can get better deals and be more selective.

Keep in mind that since the MLS is a database, search criteria can be created with an agent/broker (or other online service) to find specific types of deals you are interested in buying. These can be set up where any new or updated listing matching your criteria can be sent to you automatically in an email, so you don't have to go through the MLS every day looking for deals. Set some alerts based on criteria that you want, and when you get an email start analyzing the deal.

Buying a Deal Listed On the MLS

So how do you buy a deal you are interested in that's on the MLS? Great question. Properties listed on the MLS are being marketed by the agent/broker who listed them. You will need to contact the agent or broker directly or use your own agent to make an offer. When the market turned down, I had three investor agents who I worked with and made offers. Most offers were not accepted, but I did get some of them, and still own them today as rentals.

WHOLESALERS

Earlier in the book we discussed selling wholesale. However, you can also buy wholesale. A wholesaler will put a deal under contract from someone at a lower price, and sell to you (the buyer) at a higher price. This can happen either through an assignment of contract from the wholesaler or via a contract directly with the wholesaler. A wholesaler is basically a middleman that can find deals for you.

I have purchased many deals from wholesalers, and I have also wholesaled many deals myself to other investors. In fact, early in my real estate career, I wholesaled property for a couple of years for income and to build cash for buying deals. Since this is the second tier, you can theoretically get better deals from a wholesaler than you can through the MLS. This means that you can generally get more equity from a wholesaler than you can directly from the MLS. As I stated earlier, there are no absolutes here, and markets can vary drastically. The point is to help you understand this in a much clearer manner.

Finding a Good Wholesaler

To find deals here, you need to find a wholesaler and get on their email list. You will have more success if you build a personal relationship with a few wholesalers over time and have them treat you as a "pocket buyer" (meaning they call you as soon as they have a deal and ask if you want to buy it). This takes not only time but, most importantly, experience closing at least one transaction with them. There has to be a mutual trust established to make this work effectively.

Once you are on a wholesaler's list, you will get a lot of emails and/or calls. Once those emails/calls start rolling in, you are going to see all kinds of offers from different wholesalers. As always, don't believe everything you read or hear. Often times, wholesalers misrepresent deals. So as you start to look at the properties they send, I want you to be cautious about anything that looks too good to be true, and to carefully evaluate wholesalers who tend to make such claims.

Words of Caution about Wholesalers

As you start to work with wholesalers, be careful when dealing with them. Not all of them are created equal. Many wholesale deals advertised are overestimated on the value and underestimated on the repairs.

Not every wholesaler does this, but many of the "deals" I see are not deals. Many of the wholesalers are not even investors and don't know anything about real estate. You will probably know more about real estate than they do after reading a couple of chapters in this book (no joke).

A sure sign that you are working with a wholesaler you ought to avoid is that they apply a lot of undue pressure to convince a prospective buyer to put up a non-refundable deposit. I have seen these "deposits" as high as $7,500. If you don't close, they will keep the money!

So do your due diligence. If you are not confident in the numbers, let someone else buy it. Ask yourself:

- Have you run your own comps on this deal or have you had an appraiser, agent, or other expert analyze the ARV for you?

- Have you had the property measured (in our market we see over 25% of the tax roll data wrong on square footage)?

- Are you confident that the scope of work/repair/rehab number is accurate?

If you answered no to any of these questions, you need to walk away from this deal. There will be other deals, so don't be pressured into buying anything.

Now, sometimes wholesalers make mistakes that actually work to your advantage. I have witnessed wholesalers miscalculate their numbers in the opposite direction. They looked at the wrong comps and the investor got an amazing deal. It can happen to anyone so be sure not to overlook something that might end up being one of the best deals you will ever buy.

SUMMARY

So utilizing the MLS and wholesalers are two practical ways to find deals. Finding them on the MLS is purely a function of the market. Using wholesalers is a great way to buy because you don't have to rely on your own marketing to find deals. You can work with a wholesaler to do that for you. Of course you will pay a bit more than getting the deal directly yourself, which brings us to our next topic: Buying direct.

CHAPTER 16

BUYING DIRECT

The third and final way for finding deals is what I call buying direct. This includes any deal that is contracted by you directly with the seller/owner of record of a property.

I really want to take the time to focus specifically on this because it has been the most effective method I have used to find great deals. In fact, I have made more money buying direct than all other methods combined. Whether you are flipping, wholesaling, or keeping the properties for rentals, you will generally get the best deals buying direct.

Now, when I was getting started, the Yellow Pages were filled with We Buy Houses ads, along with the newspaper (and I'm sure in some markets they are still a great advertising tool). However, the trend is that these will disappear at some point as fewer and fewer people use them as a viable advertising medium, especially in a major metropolitan area. Why? The online presence of house buyers has only gotten bigger and more competitive. Just Google "house buyers" for your area and see how many pop up.

Overall, in today's market, Internet marketing is probably a great way to go if you can find the resources that can get you the results you desire. If you are a tech savvy person and understand the power of using SEO (search engine optimization) to get you ranked on the first page of Google when someone searches "sell my house now" or "homebuyers in <name your town>", then this is an area worth pursuing.

There are many Internet marketing firms out there, and you will have to find the one that works for you for what you are trying to accomplish. I have some investor friends and clients who have hired these types of companies, and they have gotten deals. If you are interested in this method for finding deals, I would suggest you do a Google search for Internet marketing companies, and try to find one that can assist you.

As the Internet continues to evolve in terms of how people use it and what they use it for, so will the methods for marketing and advertising. For now, I want to cover the methods of buying direct that are proven effective based on my personal experience.

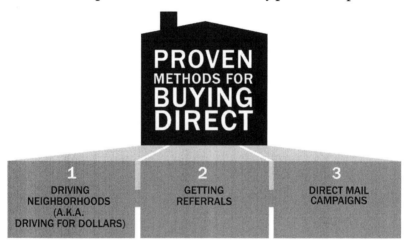

DRIVING NEIGHBORHOODS

Absolutely one of the most underrated methods for finding deals is driving neighborhoods. Why? The reason this can be so effective (especially your specific neighborhood) is it lets you target the situation/opportunity before anyone else does.

One of the best stories I know is from a client of mine who drove his neighborhood and found a vacant house that looked like it needed a lot of work. He sent a letter to the owner and after some negotiating, purchased a $279,000 house for $125,000. It needed $65,000 in work. You don't need a calculator to know this is an incredible deal. The numbers speak for themselves.

With that said, I don't know what it is about this technique that makes investors not do it. I think sometimes you can almost be blinded by a deal that's right in front of your face. Or maybe they are thinking that it's probably not a deal anyway. How do you know if you don't engage? Sometimes the easiest and least expensive way of doing something can give a false impression of its effectiveness. It's certainly the easiest method, and for that reason alone, I think many investors overthink it and assume it's not worth doing. Don't make this mistake!

How to Drive a Neighborhood

The best way to do this is to just drive around your area or an area where you want to buy real estate deals, and look for the ugliest house. It will be easy to spot because it will have one or more of the following:

- Tall grass and weeds
- Peeling paint
- All the lights off all the time
- Trash or furniture in the yard
- Uncollected newspapers or mail
- Or just a general look of vacancy

In the story just mentioned about my client who found the $279K house for $125K, there was furniture on the curb set for bulk trash pickup. If you have one of these houses, do the following as soon as you can:

1. Find the owner of record. This is easy to do online either through the tax roll data for the county or some other public records source.

2. Talk to the neighbors and find out what's going on with the house. They don't need to know what you are trying to do. You'd be surprised how many will

tell you everything you need to know including how to contact the owner.

3. Send the owner a letter saying you are interested in buying the house and can close quickly or try to find their phone number and contact them.

Does this sound like a lot of work? Not when you consider it could be worth $67,000 in net profit like what my client made. Set a goal to drive your targeted neighborhood each week for the next 12 months and repeat the above steps 1–3. Hey, if you don't have the budget for a direct-mail campaign and don't have anyone referring you deals yet, this should be your method of buying direct!

GETTING REFERRALS

Getting deals through referrals can be less complicated and deliver some of the best equity deals you will ever get. Think about this for a minute, how many things have you received that were from a referral? You may have found your job through a referral, your clients through referral, or maybe even met your spouse through a referral. So many things in life come from referrals—house deals are no different.

Get Creative

Over time, I have encouraged investors to utilize all of the resources available to them when finding deals, and one of the best ways again and again has been through referrals. So, tell the people in your network (or mastermind group) that you are looking for a distressed house to buy.

Notice that I did not say, "Tell everyone you are going to start investing in real estate." We already went over why that's not a good idea.

I have had clients find deals in the strangest ways, from their dentist's mother-in-law, to their barber, from having a drink next to someone at a bar, to a Facebook referral. A deal I found a while back came from my exterminator. He was treating my house, knew what I was looking for, and turned me on to a great deal. I could go on and on, but you get my point. You really don't have any excuses for not finding a deal until you've tried all the things I just mentioned.

Talk to Neighbors

You will find that as you are working on a house (i.e., performing the rehab/remodel), neighbors may stop by to see what's happening. I have had several clients of mine find deals on the same street because someone came by and said that they would like to sell their house as well.

Also, there are neighbors who will stop by and walk around inside while work is being done. It's natural. Don't get frustrated or upset because you think they are being nosy or trespassing. They may be the person on the street who knows everything that is going on in the neighborhood, and you absolutely want to get to know them. They can check on the house for you when your contractors are not there. They can offer you insight into the history of the neighborhood if they have lived there for a long time. But most importantly, they can tell you who else might be in a situation where they need to sell. This type of neighbor knows those around them and their personal situations. Maybe there is someone getting divorced, moving into a senior center, or had a death in the family. All of these situations can create opportunity for you as a real estate investor. Take advantage and be proactive. Ask them if they know about any houses that might be worth a knock on the door or other form of contact.

Imagine you tell people you are looking for a distressed house to buy (and nothing more). If they know someone needing to get out of their situation, have them give you a call. Or, better yet, get their number and see if you can contact them (after a warm introduction). There are many ways to find referrals and make them work. Remember the potential for huge deals here. Always follow up.

DIRECT-MAIL CAMPAIGNS

Absolutely the BEST deals I have ever purchased came from a direct-mail campaign. I could go on and on again here, but let me instead give you a few quick examples:

Example #1: I once bought a deal for $100 that was worth $85,000 (no I am not joking). It needed $40,000 in work. With $45,000 in equity and $850/mo in rent, it was a great deal with multiple investing strategies available (could be wholesaled, retailed, or rented). I still have it as a rental.

Example #2: I bought another deal worth $190,000 for $56,000. It needed $63,000 in work. With $71,000 in equity, it made for an amazing deal. I sold that deal retail after it had been rented for a few years.

Example #3: I purchased a house for $13,000 that needed $27,000 in work. ARV was $85,000. I cash flowed this property for several years and then sold it for a nice profit.

I'm providing you with these examples so you can see the power of a direct-mail campaign. It's because of the ability to find deals like these that I still believe direct mail is, at least for now, the best way to find the best deals. It may not always be this way, but it will be for the foreseeable future, despite the changing technology and greater percentage of marketing and advertising being done online. There is something about holding a physical letter or postcard that makes it personal and gets a seller's attention. A letter is especially effective but postcards work as well.

Preparing a Direct-mail Campaign

As it sounds, a direct-mail campaign involves sending letters and/or postcards in the mail directly to prospective sellers. You might think sending something just to say "We Buy Houses" is a waste of time because no one reads "junk mail," right? Well, not everyone throws it in the trash. Some people do read such cards, and will call you, at which point you will need to qualify the deal.

I have had calls from people who have saved my letter or postcard for five years! Why keep it so long? At the bottom of the message it says to "Keep this with your important real estate documents," or, "Not ready to sell? Keep this card for future reference." YES! This type of messaging can and will have an impact simply because it asks someone to take action. The point here is direct mail is something that builds upon itself, meaning the more you do it, the better the results you are going to have.

Consistency is the Key

So direct mail does work, but it requires consistency. It cannot be emphasized enough here that without consistency, you will NOT have ongoing success with direct mail. I have done many direct-mail campaigns over the years and know this from first-hand experience. So I really want to drive it into your head that when I say "campaign," I genuinely mean a series of organized mailers intended to drive call volume from qualified sellers where deals can be made. It's vitally important to understand that this is not a one-time event.

The most effective way to implement a direct-mail campaign is to mail to the same group multiple times (four to five times) with a different message each time. For example, you might take a list of 5,000 (or any manageable number where you can handle the call volume) and set up a letter/postcard to go out every four to six weeks over the course of five to seven months.

The Cost of a Direct-mail Campaign

I better point this out now because you are certainly thinking about this and probably have since the first sentence of this section. How much does this cost to do? First, let me say that direct-mail campaigns do cost money and are based on the size of the campaign. You will need to have money budgeted to initiate and pursue an effective direct-mail campaign, and it is important to have this cost identified before you ever start doing it.

The worst thing you can do is a single mail campaign. You might as well not do any at all. What if you do and get a couple of solid deals? That can absolutely happen! However, if you don't get any, you will probably become extremely frustrated and want to quit altogether. The reality is you may not see a higher volume of deals until the fourth or fifth mailer, so you will need to stay focused and keep the campaign going.

Letters and Postcards: Two Different Types of Direct-Mail Campaigns

Let's look at the two different types of campaigns I have implemented over the years so you can get a better understanding of them. Letter campaigns cost more money than postcard campaigns, however letter campaigns produce a higher call volume than postcard campaigns. Higher call volume means more deals. It's a pure numbers game. The more you put out there consistently, the better your return.

Costs are going to change over time in terms of postage and mail processing, but a first-class postage Forever stamp, as of this writing, costs $.47, and if you multiply that by 5,000 letters, you get a postage total of $2,350. That does not include the paper, envelopes and mail processing cost. What's mail processing? Mail processing involves printing, folding, stuffing, sorting, addressing, stamping and even delivering the mail to the post office. I just got a quote so I could put it in this book as an example for you. For letter processing the cost is $1,325.90, which includes dropping it off at the post office. So, the total cost with postage for 5,000 letters would be $2,350 (postage) + $1,325.90 (processing) = $3,675.90 as of this writing using a mail processing center here in Dallas. For 5,000 postcards, total cost is around $1,937. This may vary with which company you use, but I wanted to at least give you an example.

But wait a minute. Can't you do this yourself? You can, but not at a high volume. If you did 1000 letters, that's a lot of manual labor when machines can do this so much faster and more efficiently. You doing this yourself is equivalent to you picking up that hammer or paintbrush and working on that house you are going to flip. Are you in the mail processing business or are you a real estate investor?

Focus on finding deals and not processing mail for your campaign. There are processing centers that do this as a business. How do you find them? Do a Google search for mail processing in your city/town. You just send them your file of names and addresses and they will do everything else including taking the mail to the post office.

Consider Spacing Out Your Mailings Over a Week

With that said, I am okay with you making one change to the processing list mentioned in the above paragraph. You can take the letters or postcards to the post office. Why? You may not be able to handle the call volume depending on your schedule, and it's more cost effective to process a larger amount of mail at one time. If you mail 5,000 letters, your phone is going to be ringing. You can be certain of that. If it's not ringing (sometimes the following day depending on where they are being mailed), your campaign was not sent. So you may want to space it out a bit and mail 1,000 to 2,000 at a time over the course of a week.

What to Expect

How many calls can you expect to get from a letter campaign versus a postcard campaign? Letters can generate 1%+ call volume on average over time depending on your market, the time of the month, the time of the year, and how good your list is. Postcards can generate up to half of 1% over time, also depending on your market, the time of the month, the time of the year, and how good your list is. This means all of the calls don't come in right away, but a good percentage of them come in the first two weeks after your campaign is sent, and then taper off after that.

Let's say you send 2,000 letters to a very targeted list, and over three weeks you get 15 calls. If you get one deal out of this, it's absolutely worth it. If you get two deals out of it, throw yourself a victory party because these are excellent results! This same letter campaign can produce calls and deals much later because someone will hang on to your letter and call you six months from now when something has changed and they are ready to sell.

Over time in my experience, I would say that on average 1 in 18 calls is a deal. That means it would take roughly 18 calls for me to get a deal that I could do something with and make money (i.e., wholesale it, flip it retail, or keep it as a rental).

Does that mean you should expect the same numbers? NO. Your volume may differ dramatically, and you won't know what it will be until you execute your own campaign in your selected market.

Sometimes the first call you get is a deal and that can ruin you. What? Yes, I am serious. In the beginning if you get a deal right out of the gate, like in your first few calls, it has the potential to make you jaded. By that I mean you may think that you are really good at this direct mail stuff, and/or that this is just super easy. I have seen it many times. None of this is true by the way, you just happened to hit someone at the right time (which is all this type of advertising is designed to do) and got lucky with it being this quick.

What's even worse when this happens is you stop marketing – which is a big mistake! I'm telling you I have seen it happen when an investor gets two deals and thinks, "Wow, I cannot handle any more right now so I'm going to slow down the marketing," only to figure out that when they start back up again it took three more mailers to get another deal. Don't be that investor! Guess what? This happened to me and you can read about it in Chapter 18.

Executing Mail Campaigns

Alright, now let's go over what specifically will need to be done as you execute your direct-mail campaign. This is important stuff, so I want to be sure you get the process down.

Step 1: Establish a Budget for Your Campaign
Direct-mail campaigns require an investment in capital. It can be a significant amount of capital depending on the size of your campaign. As discussed, you will need to calculate the cost for everything involved (i.e., the data for your list, paper, postcards, printing, postage, sorting, delivery, etc.).

Step 2: Get a Solid List of Names and Addresses

You want both the owner's address and the property's address. Just remember, "garbage in, garbage out." If you have good data, your campaign has the potential to be good. If you have bad data, you will get no calls and no leads/deals. There are lots of sources here, but I find the tax roll data of a particular municipality (i.e., county, city, etc.) to be the best source.

I have found public records work best because they are easier to obtain and contain most of the critical data you need. They can usually be purchased directly from the municipality, or there are services that take the public records and will format them any way you like.

For example, in North Texas, you can get Dallas County, Denton County, Collin County, and Tarrant County data directly from the source. Or you can use a service like www.TaxNetUSA. com to get the data in a specific format with certain fields that may or may not be available from the county data. Services like this cost money, but nothing unreasonable and definitely worth the money. I think the last list I purchased was from TaxNetUSA for Dallas County and was $400. There are other lists that can be used as well, such as foreclosure listings and probate listings:

- The foreclosure list in a mail campaign is a one-time mail list. In the Dallas/Fort Worth market covering four major counties, you can buy these lists from foreclosure listing services (just Google that phrase).

- Probate listings are posted each day and there are services that provide this data as well. Personally, I do not market to these lists, but they can be effective.

Step 3: Refine Your List

Don't stop there, keep working on your list to make it better:

- Filter your data. The more you can shrink the list the more targeted it becomes and the more cost effective. What should you look for in terms of filtering? I have created several different types of lists that I have used over time. Two of the most successful for me were (1) non-owner occupied houses (owner does not live at the property address I am targeting), and (2) any home owned for more than 20 years (potential for equity here is much higher).

- Shrink the list further with year built, square footage, and location. In other words, query for a specific subset that matches what you are looking for, like all houses owned for 20 years+, with > 1,000 square feet, built after 1978, owned by a natural person (not an entity), in specific cities in Dallas County. This type of filtering creates a more manageable list. You can get even more granular than this if you like. I have found it easier to get this in some kind of comma delimited text that can be imported into a spreadsheet and used in a mail merge.

Step 4: Decide on Letters vs. Postcards

As I mentioned above, letters give a statistically higher call response. I found that using a real postage stamp as opposed to a postage indicium (see image) from a mail processor gets better results.

PRSRT STD
U.S. Postage
PAID
U.S. Press
31601

Your mail processor will more than likely have one of these, and the post office will charge them a different rate (lower) if they are presorted in the manner they are to be delivered. Basically, when you see mail like this, you assume immediately that it's junk mail. You want to avoid this because most of these will go in the trash. Your goal is to get every letter opened. Use a real stamp even if it costs a bit more.

On the other hand, postcards can get up to 1/2% call back. I like to go with the bulk rate presorted mail, and am fine with using a postage indicium, as opposed to using a postcard stamp. A postcard obviously does not have to be opened and you can have a great message on it that gets the viewer's attention. See the sample postcard in the Appendix (Item 2.B).

Step 5: Create the Appropriate Content

For postcards, "We Buy Houses" is very specific and will make your message clear. You can create variations of this, but do not say, "We Buy Ugly Houses" as that is a registered trademark, and HomeVestors will send you a nasty letter from their legal team asking you to cease and desist if they discover the letter. I know people who have received letters from them, so don't do this.

You might also include "any condition/any situation," or something along those lines. It also needs to have your phone number. Letters can say the same thing. I have done this in a mail merge format where I write one letter that is going to everyone and the merge fields are their name, mailing address and property address.

For an example, see the sample letter in the Appendix (Item 2.A).

Step 6: Put Your Campaign on Autopilot

Once you have everything in place, contact your mail processing center. Try to have the different letters or postcards ready for them to run at different intervals. There are many ways to do this, but work something out with them that will get your mail processed and sent every four to six weeks over the course of five months or so. Maybe call them ahead of time when you are ready to initiate the next round and make sure they are ready to go. The best advice I can give you here is to be sure you manage your mail processor.

Step 7: Qualify and Track Each Call

We'll cover this more thoroughly elsewhere, but it is important to track each call both in terms of number of calls and the results of the call. You can do it manually, or with a lead generation tool online to track your leads and appointments. For instance, Propelio.com offers a free lead tracking solution (at least, as of this writing) which might be something to consider if you are looking for a place to get started.

Step 8: Get the Deal(s) Under Contract!

You will need to find a contract form that you can use that a title company is going to be able to accept. Contract forms can vary by state, so find out the best form to use in your state by either talking to your agent/broker or attorney. You want something that you can use over and over again. In Texas, the TREC (Texas Real Estate Commission) governs the forms, and anyone is allowed to use them. Check to see how it works in your state.

Step 9: Repeat Step 1 through 8 Until Your List Needs to be Updated/Refreshed

I would do this at least once a year. Remember, each mailer in a campaign needs a different message on the letter or postcard. It is important to change the message and not the list. For example, "We Buy Houses," followed by the next letter or postcard message, which would maybe say, "I Want to Buy Your House for Cash," or something along those lines. Be sure to alter the content of the letter or postcard as well.

Keys for Improving Your Direct-mail Campaigns

I briefly touched on this above, and believe it is important enough to reiterate again. I have seen a couple of things happen with investors when doing direct-mail campaigns, and I don't want to see you make the same mistakes they made:

1. Some investors will send a mailer, get responses, not get any deals, falsely determine that it must not be working, and decide to stop the campaign. This is a big mistake! If you send a sizeable list (i.e., 1,000+), you should get some calls right away, ensuring that your list did go out the door. Even if the calls are "Take me off your list," you know it was at

least mailed. If you don't get any calls, you might check your list again to make sure it wasn't bad data. Smaller lists, of course, have lower call volume. Also, check to make sure the phone number is correct!

2. Conversely, and as I mentioned above, I have seen investors have success right away and start working multiple deals (Hey, it happens, and it's great when it does!). Unfortunately, they get so overwhelmed that they stop marketing. Never stop mailing during a campaign! Those letters/postcards need to go out the door every interval that you have established. You will get residual calls from prior mailings (i.e., you will get a call from your first mailer when your fourth one is being mailed). Sometimes you will not see enough deals until your fifth mailer, which is another reason why it is so critical to stay consistent.

REVIEWING SOURCES FOR DEALS

Wow! That was a lot to digest, I know. Stay with me here, and don't get overwhelmed. Make a plan and focus on one or more of these proven methods, and you will absolutely see results. Just to recap what we discussed in Chapters 15 and 16:

1. **The MLS:** Depending on market conditions this can be a great resource for finding deals. Alerts can be set where all you have to do is check your inbox. Typically, you will pay more for a deal on the MLS than you will for a deal purchased either wholesale or direct, but it is definitely worth including as part of your overall strategy for finding deals.

2. **Wholesalers:** If you can rely on someone else to bring you deals that you don't have to find yourself, it's absolutely worth getting on some wholesalers' lists, and have them email or call you when they find something. You will generally pay more for a deal than buying direct (as they are the middleman), but you can buy excellent deals from wholesalers, and they should not be overlooked.

3. **Buying Direct:** Definitely the best way to find the best deals. It costs money to do direct mail, but getting referrals and driving neighborhoods cost nothing except time, and will definitely pay off for you if worked correctly. Theodore Roosevelt said, "Do what you can, with what you have, where you are." I couldn't agree more.

My Advice

I would start by getting some alerts set in the MLS (or have your agent/broker do this for you). I would go to some meetings or go online to find some wholesalers in your area and get on their list if, for nothing else, just to see what they have for sale. This costs you nothing, and you can get some experience analyzing deals. Who knows, you may find a deal that you want to buy, but do your due diligence.

When it comes to buying direct, I would start driving some targeted neighborhoods and telling people what you are looking to buy. Just doing these two things will be productive, and you should feel good that you have taken these steps along with the alerts and getting on wholesaler lists.

If you have the budget, launch that direct-mail campaign and stick to it.

With all of these things in place, your inbox is going to start getting emails, and your phone will start to ring, which leads me to ask the following question, "What do you do when your phone starts ringing and you have a seller ready to talk to you about their situation?

Qualify the deal, which happens to be the subject of the next chapter.

CHAPTER 17

QUALIFYING A DEAL

So a neighbor called you because they heard you buy houses. Or, you sent a 3,000-piece mail campaign, and your phone is ringing. What do you do now?

Not to worry. When dealing with/talking to a seller/owner of record, you must have two things present to make the property you are evaluating a "deal." Those two things are seller motivation and equity in the property.

I want to spend this chapter covering the process you'll go through when you talk to a seller from the perspective of motivation and equity. Let's go through it one piece at a time.

MOTIVATION AND EQUITY

Why must the seller have both motivation and equity? Consider the following examples:

- **Example One:** A seller is getting divorced and needs to move ASAP. However, the house is worth $250,000 and she owes $240,000. There is no equity in this deal although there is lots of motivation. She cannot afford to sell at a price where you can buy.

- **Example Two:** You have a seller who has a house worth $180,000 that they own free and clear; however, there is no compelling event making them sell the house. In fact, they are just seeing what they could get for it, and decided to call you. If you have equity and no motivation, there is no deal.

- **Example Three:** A seller inherited a house after the passing of his parents. He lives out of town and desperately needs money because he has been out of work for over a year. He decides to call you after receiving your letter and wants to close next week. The house is owned free and clear, and he is willing to accept any offer at this point just to get some money. Here you have motivation and equity and definitely a deal you need to pursue.

Building Rapport

When you take a call from a seller, it's important to build rapport with them. This means try to make a connection by empathizing with their situation by putting yourself in their shoes. Remember, being sincere is fundamental to every situation with a seller (or anyone for that matter), and being a good listener is absolutely critical. Your objective is to quickly set their expectations.

After you introduce yourself and get a feel for how the call is going to go, it's critical that you mention you invest in real estate to make a profit before asking any questions. Why? This sets a tone (as well as expectations) with the seller that you are not doing this for fun (although it can be very fun and exciting to work deals). It lets them know that this is a business, and you are here to make money. The wording you use is up to you. "I buy and sell real estate for a profit," is perfectly fine. Once you get a feel for the seller's personality and attitude, it will be easier to come up with the right words.

BE PREPARED WITH A CALL SHEET OR SCRIPT

Now, in order to be as effective as possible at building the rapport you need, before you take that call, you'll need some type of call sheet or script to capture as much information as possible. As a long time software/technology guy, I always had the tendency to use an electronic system to capture information. While this is great if you have a headset on your phone and can type the responses into a form online, it might be best to create a call sheet in a notebook, and fill out the page manually as you get the information from the seller.

The important thing is that you find a way that works for you to capture the data easily. Don't think you have to fill the sheet out in order, just fill it in as you find out the information, leave blanks and jump around—it's fine. In fact, if you have a paper form in front of you, those blanks will stare back at you, making it easier to make sure you cover everything.

You may be uncomfortable because you are not good in this area or have difficulty talking to people about anything business related. If you are in that camp, my advice for you is just be yourself. Don't try to come across as a big business person or fake who you are. That can be the kiss of death, and most people who call you are going to be able to detect if you are for real or not. They don't want to waste time with someone they think is shady, and won't close. Be warm and personable and just talk to them like you would a friend. Be their friend and be a good listener. People do business with people they like, and sellers will do business with you if they like you. If they don't like you, they are probably going to hang up and call someone else.

SAMPLE QUESTIONS TO ASK A SELLER

Now, to help even more, I have included some important questions that you should ask the seller. I did not, however, organize them in any particular order. Think of this as a list of questions you could ask, depending on how a particular call is going.

So the way to succeed here is to develop your ability to gauge the overall attitude/sense of urgency with the seller. Sometimes this means go with the flow of the call. Some sellers are going to get right to the point, while others will take forever to get your questions answered. The key is to be patient with everyone if you want to get an appointment to see the house, which should be the goal of every call when there is motivation and equity. There is no reason to waste your time or the seller's time by setting an appointment to perform any due diligence if both of these do not exist. Politely explain to the seller that you will not be able to help them and move on to the next lead.

Learn to Listen More than You Talk

There's an old saying that you have two ears and one mouth for a reason. Seriously, think about it from that perspective. This can be hard, but getting good at this is definitely worth it. Sometimes just letting someone talk will allow you to fill in the blanks without having to ask any questions. This lets every conversation be unique and organic. Be open to that and you'll do great with this list of questions.

A sales director I used to work for, who was a phenomenal salesperson, always practiced golden silence. For him, this meant to wait a few seconds after someone responds before you say anything. This takes practice, as you do not want to do this in a scripted way where you make someone feel uncomfortable. Just remember to not talk over anyone as you are listening to them. If you feel the seller is pressed for time, try to get as many questions answered that relate to motivation and equity as you can.

Alright, here are the questions. Again, don't worry about the order here. Use what you need when you need it based upon your conversation:

SAMPLE QUESTIONS TO ASK A SELLER

VERIFY CONTACT INFORMATION

- WHAT IS YOUR NAME?
- WHAT IS YOUR PHONE NUMBER?
- HOW DID YOU HEAR ABOUT US?

DETERMINE MOTIVATION

- WHAT MADE YOU DECIDE TO SELL?
- HOW LONG HAVE YOU OWNED THE HOUSE?
- WHAT HAPPENS IF YOU DON'T SELL IT?
- HOW LONG HAS IT BEEN FOR SALE?
- HAVE YOU RECEIVED ANY OFFERS ON IT?
  (IF YES, PLEASE PROVIDE DETAILS)
- HAVE YOU FOUND ANOTHER HOUSE TO MOVE TO?
  (IF THIS IS THEIR CURRENT RESIDENCE)

ABOUT THE HOUSE

- WHAT IS THE ADDRESS OF THE PROPERTY?
- BEDROOMS? BATHS? GARAGE? YEAR BUILT? SQFT? CENTRAL HVAC?
- ARE THERE ANY ADDITIONS TO THE HOUSE?
- WHAT IS THE CONDITION OF THE HOUSE?
- DO YOU LIVE THERE?
- IS THE HOUSE VACANT/OCCUPIED?
- IF VACANT, HOW LONG?
- IF RENTED, HOW MUCH IS THE RENT AND WHAT ARE THE LEASE TERMS?

UNDERSTANDING THE VALUE

- WHAT DO YOU FEEL THE HOUSE IS WORTH?
- HOW DID YOU COME UP WITH THAT VALUE?
- IF I PAY YOU ALL CASH, WHAT IS THE BEST PRICE YOU CAN GIVE ME?
- IF I PAY YOU CASH AND WE CLOSE NEXT WEEK, WHAT'S THE BEST PRICE YOU CAN GIVE ME?

UNDERSTANDING THE FINANCING

- WHAT IS THE MORTGAGE BALANCE?
- IS YOUR MORTGAGE CURRENT/BEHIND?
- IF BEHIND, HOW MUCH?
- HAVE YOU RECEIVED A NOTICE OF FORECLOSURE FROM YOUR LENDER?

Once you start getting some of these questions completed, you should start to be able to determine if there is a deal there or not. Be sure to put the date and time of the call at the top of the sheet so you can have this for future reference. Also, keep a log of any activity on this sheet as you continue to work this particular lead, such as any viewing appointments, if/when you are mailing them an offer, etc.

If you believe this might be a deal and you want to move forward, you will want to set expectations with the seller over the phone that you will need to see the house to determine the cost and scope of work in order for you to make an offer. Also, make it clear that you may be making them an offer on the spot based on what the numbers look like. We will discuss making offers in the next chapter.

If your call goes well and you get an appointment to see the house, be sure to get your contractor(s) involved immediately because, as we discussed earlier, the clock is ticking!

GETTING ACCESS

If you are wholesaling, you may want to get buyers and contractors inside to see the house, and it is my advice that you get permission to access the property from the seller if you have agreed on price and can put this language in the contract. You may need to get your contractor in as well. If the house is vacant, there should not be an issue. However, if the house is occupied, you are going to need to coordinate this with the occupant (whether tenant or owner).

Some words of caution on occupied houses. If the subject property is owner-occupied that presents a different scenario than if it is tenant-occupied. We need to spend some time here so you can understand what you need to do to make your deal work without any issues.

Owner-Occupied Properties

An owner-occupied house needs to be completely vacant on or before closing as part of the contract. You will want to drive by the house prior to closing to make sure the seller has vacated the premises.

If they haven't, and it is in your contract that the property needs to be vacated prior to closing, then my advice is don't close! It is critical that you have this written in the contract, especially if you are new in the business. Why? If you are wholesaling this deal, your buyer is not going to want to deal with someone who will not vacate and might have to be evicted. If you are keeping this deal for yourself to flip or rent, you will delay your rehab, and this will cost you time and money.

If this situation occurs, evicting an owner occupant, or former owner occupant, can be very difficult. Doing a seller's temporary lease back is more than likely governed by the laws in your state. In Texas, a standard TREC (Texas Real Estate Commission) contract has an addendum that provides for this up to a certain period of time. You will need to check with your state's laws on this.

If the owner of the house is still living there, it is important to ask if they have another place to move to at or before closing. If they don't have another place to move, then you may want to hold off on closing until they do.

When you are negotiating a deal with the seller, be sure to set the expectation that you are going to need to get your contractor and possibly an appraiser inside, and that you will try to schedule this for the same day. If you are wholesaling this house, you may want to bring a buyer with you to see it. You should have the deal under contract with the seller, with a memorandum recorded as discussed earlier, before you take your buyer with you to see the house.

Tenant-Occupied Properties

When a house you are buying is tenant occupied, you need to determine what is going on with that situation. When you are negotiating a deal with the seller, you need to make sure that the tenant situation is also being addressed in the contract. Situations like moving out, being evicted, or wanting to stay. Whatever the case is, be sure you understand it before moving forward, so there are no surprises before or after closing.

If the property is going to stay as a rental property, and you intend to wholesale it like that, you will want to get approval from the seller and the tenant that you will have access to the property. This does not mean you need to tell the seller that you intend to sell this to another investor. In my opinion it's none of their business what you are going to do with it.

As you can probably imagine, telling the seller that you are in fact not the one buying the property, might blow up your deal. Don't look at this as being devious in some sort of malicious way. You are simply working two deals that are independent of one another. Just know this—to commit to the deal with an executed contract, you are going to need further access to get your contractor and prospective buyers inside. You will also want to get a copy of the lease for review (if one exists).

There are many buyers looking for situations like this where they can have a tenant in place. However, if the owner is selling the property because the tenant hasn't paid rent in six months, you may not want to put a contract on the property. If/when you are new in the business, I understand you not wanting to move forward. However, over time you will get more experience, and if the deal is priced right, you will absolutely take it and deal with the tenant situation either before or after closing.

Squatter Occupied Properties

Oh yes, squatters can create a motivated seller faster than you can say the word. So what's a squatter? Good question. A squatter is any occupant living in a property without permission. That's correct. They are living there without the permission of the owner of record and, of course, without a lease in place.

So can't you just call the police and get them out of there? Not necessarily. You need to understand that squatters can have certain rights, and the laws are different in every state. You need to discuss this with an experienced real estate attorney before you sign a contract.

More than likely, you may not be able to get inside the property because the squatter will not let you in. This is a situation where you must deal with them in order to get the deal. Consider this complication when making your offer. The price has to be "right" which means it's going to be a much lower offer than if there were no squatter there. I would personally take on a situation like this because I know what the laws are in my state, and if I could get clear title and have to deal with this squatter, that's not a problem for me.

Sometimes the squatter is an heir that is making a claim to the property. I have seen other situations where the squatter claims to have permission from the owner when they actually don't have permission. The point here is you may not be able to get them out of the property quickly. This is probably why the seller is calling you to get rid of this headache. You may be the best hope for them in this situation. Keep this in mind as this is a key point I want to make: *you are a problem solver for motivated sellers*, and that is the value you are bringing to this and other difficult situations.

This is not easy, and you will be dealing with complicated situations that involve multiple heirs. What's that old saying? Oh yes, "If it were easy, everyone would be doing it." That's exactly right. Without you stepping in, there is probably no deal to be had. But I can promise you that someone else will come along and help this seller, and they will reap all of the reward. Your best deals are sometimes the ones with the biggest problems, so don't turn away a deal just because the situation is difficult.

HANDLING "TAKE ME OFF YOUR LIST" REQUESTS

One more thing we should cover: people asking you to take them off your call list. You're going to get a lot of these types of calls. Someone gets your letter and is offended and tired of getting them. They decide to call you to get you to stop sending these.

Do you have to stop contacting them? Ultimately, it's your choice whether you want to do this or not. Some things to consider as you make that choice:

- Was the house sold? If it was sold, there is obviously no reason to continue marketing to them, and you can take them off your list.

- Will an opportunity to sell it ever materialize? Meaning, will there ever be enough motivation and equity for you to get a deal?

- Remember, just because someone doesn't like getting the mail you are sending doesn't mean they should permanently go off the list.

CHAPTER 18

SUCCESSFULLY MAKING OFFERS

A lright! Let's get some deals going!
But wait a minute. How do we get deals under contract? By making offers! Since there is a direct correlation between making offers and getting deals, we are going to discuss the importance of this, along with the process, as well as the necessary steps you need to take to do this successfully.

MAKE AS MANY OFFERS AS YOU CAN EACH MONTH

There is an old saying in real estate investing circles, "If you're not making offers, you are not going to get deals." It sounds so simple, but you would be surprised how many investors I speak with on a regular basis who say they cannot find deals.

My response is usually, "How many offers did you make this month?" Their reply is none, one, or some very small number. The bottom line is it's a numbers game, and you will need to make many offers to get a deal under contract.

How many offers does it take to get a deal under contract? It's a difficult question to answer. All I can say is make as many offers as you can until you start seeing results. These can be offers on MLS deals, offers to wholesalers, or offers directly with the owners of record of a property.

A Quick Story to Illustrate My Point

When I first started utilizing direct mail many years ago, I got very lucky and got two very good deals under contract that I was able to wholesale quickly and make money. Because of this success, I stopped talking to wholesalers and didn't make any offers on MLS deals. I also failed to follow through on some of the other direct mail leads I received because they didn't seem to be as good as the first two deals I wholesaled.

So guess what happened? I had no deals working, and my phone wasn't ringing like it did the first few weeks after I launched my direct-mail campaign. This was a big mistake and set me back a couple of months before I got my next deal. Sometimes you have to learn things the hard way, and I was certainly not an exception to this.

So, what was I thinking? Because they came so easily, I falsely made the assumption that my phone would keep ringing and I would get more deals just like the first two. I also made the rookie mistake of thinking if I make too many offers, how would I handle all of the volume if they were all accepted? It's crazy what you think might happen when you are just getting started. When neither of these things happened, I realized that I had to start making offers and do it consistently. These offers now included REOs listed on the MLS and wholesale deals. I also realized that a direct-mail campaign needs to function as a campaign and not as an isolated event.

My Advice

Just as you would set a goal for the number of deals you are going to do, or the amount of cash flow you want to make, or the profit amount you are targeting, you need a goal for the number of offers you are going to make each month because you will not reach your deal goal without an offer goal.

For example, maybe you are going to target the MLS with some alerts and make an offer on every foreclosure, every expired listing, or every distressed property that comes on the market in addition to a specific letter/postcard campaign. It doesn't matter which you pick. In fact, you could pick all of them and just make offers on everything that has potential for being a "deal."

What if you get all of them accepted? That's not going to happen, but it freaks out almost every new real estate investor. Let's assume, however, you do get all of them accepted or a majority of them accepted. First, if all of them are good deals, my advice is that you find a way to do them all. You can wholesale some, flip some, and keep some for rentals.

How do you pay for these? That's the next chapter, so stay tuned. Remember to give yourself an option period in each contract so you can exit the deal for any reason within a certain time period. This will also help you eliminate some of the unwarranted stress that you will have too many deals working (a great problem to have).

THE PROCESS FOR MAKING THE OFFER

The following are the four steps to successfully making offers to both on-market (MLS deals) and off-market sellers.

STEP 1: Determine Your Investing Strategy

After you have done your due diligence, confirmed the ARV, and have a full understanding of the scope of work required, it's time to determine which investing strategy you are going to pursue so you will know how much to offer.

There will be times when you will know before you do any due diligence what you are going to do with a specific deal, and other times when you will need all of the due diligence completed before you can make the correct decision. But when it comes to determining exactly how much you are able to offer, you must always have your due diligence completed. The investing strategy you are going to use can make a big difference in how much you are willing to offer for the deal, which brings us to the next step.

STEP 2: Determine the Offer Price

Now that you know what you are going to do with the property, you can determine the offer price. I have given you the formulas for calculating what a deal is based on each investment strategy, and as long as you have done your due diligence, you are ready to calculate the amount you are willing to pay.

With this in mind, DO NOT make any blind offers. A blind offer is when you make an offer without knowing the ARV and/or having seen the property. You or someone you trust who knows what they are doing must go and see the property in person. I don't care if you are in a competitive situation, you really like the area, or you really want this house. It doesn't matter. A physical inspection of it is required to determine your offer.

If you are still struggling with what price you should offer, find some help from another investor or your mastermind group. Discussing the numbers with a third party has helped me make the right decision on offer price many times. Let's revisit these investing strategies that we discussed in a previous chapter and how to go about making the correct offer.

Wholesale

If your plan is to wholesale the deal, you are going to need to determine how much you want to make and back into the offer from there. Use the formula discussed previously (the flipping formula) which is, 70% X ARV – Repairs = MAO, and additionally subtract the amount you want to make as an assignment fee or through a double closing.

Say you have a deal that has an ARV of $150,000 that needs $25,000 in work, and you want to make $5,000 wholesaling it. To accomplish this, you would take $150,000 X .7 - $25,000 = $80,000. If you can buy this deal for $75,000 you should absolutely be able to move this to any investor for $80,000 (or possibly more depending on market conditions). Therefore, you should offer the seller $75,000. Keep in mind that if you assign this contract you will clear $5,000.

If you have to purchase in order to double close, then you will need to make sure you take into account your closing costs for both sides of the transaction (your purchase followed by your sale) because that will lower your actual income in the deal by those amounts. To account for this, you can have your buyer pick up the tab and make them pay for all of the closing costs when you sell it to them (very common with real estate investor deals), or get the price low enough to accommodate the closing costs difference.

Flipping

Again, use the flipping formula. Your offer should not be anything over the MAO especially when you are getting started. So if you are working on the same deal above where the ARV is $150,000 and repairs (or scope of work) are $25,000, what is the maximum amount you should offer the seller? The answer is $80,000. You might be thinking, "No seller will ever take this offer." Well some will not, but some absolutely will take it. You just need to make the offer. So for flipping you can generally pay a bit more than wholesaling.

Rental Property

If you are going to keep this deal for yourself as a rental property, you need to answer the following questions and forget about the formula mentioned for flipping. We discussed these questions earlier in the book on owning Rental Property:

1. How much positive cash flow do you want?

2. How much cash-on-cash return do you want?

3. What is the amount of equity you are looking for?

4. How much are you willing to put down cash out of pocket?

You must answer these questions first to determine if it's a deal or not for you. There is no right answer here except that you need to be realistic about some of the numbers.

There is a limit to the amount of cash flow you can get because it is a function of your financing and rental amount.

However, there is no limit to cash-on-cash return. If you buy the deal right, the number is infinite (meaning you didn't have to put any money down to get the deal). You want some equity in every deal, but it's subjective.

In my opinion, never purchase a deal with negative equity. This means having enough equity to cover closing costs, any carrying costs, seller concessions, commissions, and pro-rated taxes, in case you ever needed to sell. Finally, you need to know how much cash reserves you are comfortable having after you close, to determine how much you are willing to put down.

Because rental property works differently, in many cases you can pay more than you would for a wholesale deal or a property you would flip.

Let's look at a scenario based on the numbers in the above example with an ARV of $150,000 and repairs totaling $25,000. The house will actually rent for $1,695 (over 1% of the ARV which is great). We will assume you get a 30-year mortgage, with a 4% interest rate, at a 75% LTV, with a loan amount of $112,500. Let's say property taxes are $3,500 per year and your insurance is $1,000 per year. Your monthly principal and interest payment is $537. If you add in taxes and insurance to get the monthly PITI, your total payment each month is $912. If you take $1,695 - $912 you get $783 positive cash flow. That is an amazing amount. If your interest rate were 7.5%, that would put your PITI at $1,162 and positive cash flow at $533. Still excellent.

The most effective way for you to do this is start with the results you are looking for (like we discussed in Chapter 9) and work backwards to match them to your formula.

Stay with me here because I am going to explain some things that we will cover in the chapter on financing your deals. For now, let's look at three different scenarios with three different purchase prices to calculate your cash flow, cash-on-cash return, equity, and cash out of pocket:

1. If you paid $80,000 and used a hard money loan, this will put your cash out of pocket at $6,000 including all hard money costs, your closing costs, and hazard insurance. When you refinance, you can go into a loan at

75% LTV. We will also assume you can roll your closing costs into your loan, if you completed a quality rehab and your refinance appraisal value is equal to or greater than the appraised value at the time of purchase. Your cash-on-cash return would be 156%! Yes, that is correct. Your cash flow of $783 per month X 12 / $6,000 you put down at closing = 1.56 or 156%. Think about this for a second. Where can you get 156% return on your money? You would also have about $35,000 in equity after both sets of closing costs are calculated (purchase closing costs and refinance closing costs).

2. With the same terms but a higher purchase price, if you paid $100,000 and used a hard money loan, this will put your cash out of pocket at $26,000. Your cash-on-cash return would be 36% and your equity would be $15,000. What if you paid $110,000 and used a hard money loan? This will put your cash out of pocket at $36,000. Your cash-on-cash return would be 26%. You get the idea here. However, your equity would be around $5,000, which in my opinion is too low if you needed to sell the property for some reason.

Now that you know your investing strategies, and have determined the most you are willing to pay, it's time to get your offer to the seller.

STEP 3: Put the Offer in Writing

To be a valid offer that someone is going to consider, it needs to be in writing. You might even hear a seller or a seller's agent (depending upon the deal) say, "Your verbal offer sounds great, but I need it in writing."

Just like with any business sales transaction between two parties/companies, a written contract is required because it lays out the way the transaction is to take place, all of the ground rules, as well as the price the buyer is willing to pay. Real estate contracts are no different and also need to be in writing. A written offer that is signed by both the buyer and the seller becomes a binding contract that can now move toward closing.

By submitting an offer in writing, you are formally telling the seller that you want to buy their property, under specific terms, and you are putting yourself ahead of everyone else who is not sending a written offer.

When creating the offer, be sure to include earnest money in an amount of at least 1% of the purchase price or greater. For example, if you have an offer price of $100,000, earnest money of $1,000 is probably sufficient. However, I would go much higher because I would also put in an option period that would give me the right to terminate for any reason before the option period ends.

So, if this were an offer I was making, I would put $5,000 down as earnest money. This shows you are a serious buyer, and gives the seller the confidence you are for real and going to close.

You can also add language to the contract that specifies that after the option period ends the earnest money is non-refundable for any reason other than the seller's ability to close. This means that you will relinquish the earnest money to the seller without any claim to it, once again illustrating you are a serious buyer. Let's look at the process for doing this for both on-market and off-market deals.

Property Listed on the MLS (a.k.a. On-Market Deals)

For a property listed on the MLS (an on-market deal) you are going to have to make the offer through the agent or broker who has the listing. This may or may not mean that you need an agent to submit an offer on your behalf, but that might be a good way to do it. In most situations, the seller is paying the commission (although investor deals can go differently with the buyer's agent getting paid by their buyer). Either way, just get the offer sent no matter how it needs to be submitted. If you have an agent representing you, they will have the appropriate paperwork to complete and can manage the entire transaction.

Bank owned property or other types of foreclosures (like HUD for example), are generally listed on the MLS because they want to get them market exposure. In these situations, there isn't much emotion involved because these are normally large entities with asset managers who represent the seller through a broker who has some agreement to list the asset(s) for sale.

An offer here is going to be in writing, and there will be little to no verbal communication because most of these will have instructions in the listing as to how to submit your written offer. There can be a lot of rules and some complexity as to the requirements for submitting an offer, but if you want to get this particular deal, then you are going to have to do what the seller side requires.

Off-Market Property

Find a good contract form that is acceptable to the title company you are using. They will most likely take any contract you send them, but if it's one you found on the Internet, there may be issues with them understanding it, especially if there are guidelines specific to your state that are not addressed in the actual form. Try not to get one from the Internet (unless it's from the governing body of real estate for your area on their website, and you are allowed to use it). Also DO NOT create one yourself if you are not an attorney. If you are in a state or location where you cannot get access to one, have a real estate attorney draft one that you can use.

Another way to do this is call the title company that you are going to be using, and hire their attorney to draft one for you. That is probably the easiest route to take. Obviously, the title company will have no issue using their own title company attorney's document, and you will have a form you can use for a long time.

Once you have the offer completed on the contract form, it's time to get it to the seller. This can be done in person or in the mail. I recommend *against* using email because it's too informal and doesn't have the same impact as a 9X14 inch envelope with a paper offer and cover letter.

I mentioned in the previous chapter about making offers to sellers on the spot when you meet with them. Sometimes this makes complete sense to do so and other times it does not. You will need to figure this out when you are there. If the person showing you the house is not the decision maker, I wouldn't make the offer to them unless it was required by the seller. Why? Personally, I like dealing with decision makers only, but it's not always going to be the case where you can meet with the seller. Instead, I would send this offer in the mail ASAP. Don't wait around to do this. Get the offer in the mail.

I have found that dealing with a seller/owner of record directly in an off-market situation and giving them the offer in writing or in person is one of the most effective ways to get the seller committed to a deal.

Once you and the seller sign the offer you now have an executed contract that can be sent to the title company. If a seller is out of town and you are not able to meet with them directly, verbally state your offer over the phone and follow it up with a written offer in the mail.

I include all of the following when I make an offer:

1. A cover letter explaining:
   - I will be buying all cash
   - The purchase price
   - I will pay all closing costs
   - My contact information including my phone number, mailing address, email and/or fax number where they can send the executed copy.

2. The offer in writing on the contract form that I have signed

What I want to make sure you realize is that there is something very powerful about a written offer in someone's hand, especially when the property is off-market and you are working directly with the seller/owner of record. Why is this the case? It shows professionalism and illustrates that you are serious. Most investors working with individual sellers don't do this, so you put yourself in a much better position in terms of getting the deal. Also, a written offer is the formal way to move forward in a transaction because all the seller needs to do is sign it for there to be an executed contract. I have personally seen a dramatic increase in deals I was able to get under contract (even ones

I thought I would not get) because I sent it to the seller in the mail.

Step 4: Follow Up

After an offer has been submitted, you need to determine when it's time to follow up. This can and will vary based on the types of sellers we just discussed. You want to be careful not to harass anyone or put any undue pressure on a seller that could potentially blow up any opportunity you had. However, there is a reasonable amount of time as to when you should follow up with a seller. You also don't want to submit an offer (or a bunch of offers) and never verify if they were received.

Let's consider some things to keep in mind:

Property Listed on the MLS

Your agent is going to take care of this for you and make sure that your offer was received. In most cases this will be easy for them to do because they will contact the listing agent/broker and verify. Many times, however, listing agent/brokers are difficult to reach, especially if they have multiple offers being submitted for the same deal.

It's your agent's job to manage this process. It's your job to manage your agent! Be sure to follow up with them if they haven't informed you of a status update.

Off-Market Property

After working with a seller in this situation, you have most likely had direct communication with them and may have even met them in person. Because of this, you will probably have a better feel for how this seller is going to react to your offer. If they are receptive, following up with them is going to be critical for you, if for nothing else, not losing the deal to another investor.

If you are meeting with them in person to hand them the offer, I would be sure to understand if this is a point where they are ready to sign. If they cannot sign for some reason, I would put the offer in the mail to them that same day. If you have your call sheet, it should be updated to reflect that an offer was sent in the mail and on what date. If they are local, I would follow up with them in a few days with a phone call because that should be plenty of time for them to receive the offer in the mail. If they are out of town, I would wait a week, and then call them to see if they received it and are ready to move forward.

The seller's location will determine when you need to follow up with them. You never want to appear desperate or more motivated than the seller by contacting them too early or too often.

SUMMARY

Hopefully, this chapter helped you understand the importance of making as many offers as possible and how to go about doing it. Determine your investing strategy, determine your offer price, submit the offer to the seller in writing, and follow up to move the process to closing.

CHAPTER 19

THE RISK OF BUYING MULTIPLE REAL ESTATE DEALS SIMULTANEOUSLY

Real estate investing can be exciting, especially when you get that deal you know is going to cash flow very high, or sell with a nice profit. If you are new to real estate investing, you are going to start small and build slowly—certainly the smart (and correct) move in the beginning.

However, once you fully understand all of the benefits of real estate investing, one of which is the potential to grow very quickly using leverage, you may decide to buy as many deals as you can, as fast as you can. If you fit into this profile, pay close attention to what I am saying, so you don't get burned and potentially lose money.

Whether you are buying to flip or you are building a rental portfolio, many things can happen that can hurt you and prevent you from doing other deals. Consider the following situations I have seen with many of my clients and what has prompted me to share this with you.

THE CLASSIC RENTAL SCENARIO

Ready to take it to the next level, Joe buys five houses within a 45-day time period (with three different lenders), and begins the improvements. Joe is building a rental portfolio, and these were the first five deals he has done. Although he is part of a real estate investor training group that provides coaching and mentoring to real estate investors, Joe decides to do it his own way.

Because he is new, he doesn't realize that buying this many at one time is going to prevent him from refinancing into a lower interest rate, longer term, conforming loan (like you can get from Fannie Mae). Why? His limited experience has exposed him to risk that an underwriter is going to reject. The underwriter's response to someone like this is, "Joe purchased too many properties at one time, and we are not comfortable financing them because he has no experience in the rental business."

The reality is, Joe was told by his lenders not to buy this many properties, and ended up being stuck in multiple hard-money loans paying high interest rates for over a year. After a year (meaning after 12 months of what is called "title seasoning"), the level of perceived risk by most underwriters is reduced, and Joe can try again.

At this point, he is so frustrated with the ongoing process of getting a long-term loan (by going through this same process with three other lenders, only to experience the same rejection for the same reason) that he finally goes to a small bank who is comfortable with the risk and is willing to do a single portfolio loan with all properties under one note and lien.

However, instead of getting a 30-year note with a low interest rate, they have a 15-year note with a much higher interest rate. Also, the only reason this bank is going to finance Joe's deals is because he has waited long enough, is creditworthy, and will base the financing off the value and not the purchase price (most small banks will not do a portfolio loan based on the value of the property until after 12 months). Had Joe tried this with the bank two months before, they would have either said no or would have based the loan on his cost (or value) whichever is less.

Patience Pays Off

I think you get the point here; be patient with your investing, and take it one step at a time. Be sure to get approval from a long-term lender, or a hard-money lender who works with multiple long-term lenders, and get their feedback regarding your financial situation and creditworthiness as a borrower.

It's not just credit score and income that determine your qualification. Your reserves (and experience) impact the number of deals you will be able to refinance at one time. They will be able to tell you what you are qualified for in terms of dollars as well as the number of deals you can do simultaneously.

A PAINFUL FLIPPING SCENARIO

Mary and Greg are new to real estate investing, and just completed a weekend flipper training course. They decide that they are going to rehab and flip three houses every month. Just in case you are new to this, rehabbing and flipping three houses a month is a lot! Start with a single house.

They have excellent credit and good reserves, and use leverage with hard money to finance two deals with one lender and one with another, all within 30 days. Why did they use two lenders? Their first lender was not comfortable with them doing more than two deals simultaneously and strongly advised them not to do deal three. Unfortunately, they took another path. Let's look at each deal and see what happened.

Deal 1

The rehab begins and they complete it with some subs they know (it was a very light rehab) and put it on the market. No offers yet, but they expect one soon.

After 60 days, they finally get an offer. It's also a bit lower than expected, but Mary and Greg accept it. The inspection takes place, and a list of repairs comes back that includes a roof and a hazardous electric panel that the buyer demands be replaced.

Mary and Greg didn't notice this when they purchased it from the wholesaler. In fact, they only had five minutes to make a decision to buy because there were multiple buyers ready to purchase it if they did not. It was a thin deal to begin with, and now with items they agree to fix, plus additional unforeseen closing costs, Mary and Greg get lucky and break even.

Deal 2

Mary and Greg give their contractor a check to get started and after three weeks of no work performed, start to wonder what is going on. The check cleared the bank, but their contractor cannot be found: $6,000 gone!

They find another contractor (this time a reputable one) and have to start from the beginning. They learn a lot from this experience, and from breaking even on Deal 1, and realize they better make sure this one is market ready.

Mary and Greg have to spend a bit more money than they anticipated, but believe it will pay off for them when they go to market. It does and they end up making $7,500, which is less than half of what they originally expected. The good news is they will not lose money, but will need to use all of this profit for Deal 3.

Deal 3

This turned out to be a very big project with over $40,000 in total scope of work. Unfortunately, this bid came from their first contractor who stole their money and walked off the job. After the new contractor assesses the property, he comes back with a bid of $66,000—OUCH!

Mary and Greg realize they should probably wholesale this deal as is. Unfortunately, there isn't enough room in the deal to move it, and they would have to take a $5,000 loss just to get rid of it. Against their better judgment, they decide to keep working on it.

After six months of work (and interest payments), and more than 50% over budget, Mary and Greg end up losing over $16,000, for a net loss of $8,500!

CONCLUSION

In real estate investing, anything can happen, even with the most experienced investors. However, when you are new in the business, you are exposed to more risk due to the fact that your experience is limited. What I see consistently with new investors is they overpay for real estate deals and they underestimate the true scope of work.

Overpaying for real estate deals because you are in a competitive situation is a recipe for disaster. Be patient. There will be other deals that will have better numbers. Also, never put down non-refundable earnest money unless you have done your due diligence.

Your rehab budget should have a minimum 10% buffer in it for unknowns (and the older the property, the higher that percentage should be) and be created by a reputable contractor. Failure to appropriately estimate the true costs of a rehab could cause you to be out of pocket with a significant amount of capital to cover these unforeseen costs. If you have multiple deals going on simultaneously, you could potentially be in a situation where you run out of money.

The point is start with one property and get some experience before diving in too deep by trying to rehab and flip multiple houses each month.

CHAPTER 20

FUNDING YOUR DEALS

I know what you are thinking, especially if you didn't read the table of contents. You thought I left this out of the book. Why is it here towards the end? Do I think that this is not as important or significant as the other topics in this book? Absolutely not!

Having the funds to get your deals done is critical. It's just my philosophy that if you have the right deal, you can get the money for it. How you do that is what we are going to discuss in this chapter. I also put this content at the end because I didn't want you to focus on it since a lot of people stress over this and, in most cases, for no reason.

It's important that you believe you can do any of the strategies discussed in this book, and I am counting on you having the confidence to do so. At this point you are ready to learn how to go about finding the funds for your deals.

FUNDING OPTIONS AVAILABLE FOR REAL ESTATE INVESTING

I want to cover what I believe are the top five sources for funding your deals by defining each one. Then I will address each of the investing strategies and which source(s) make the most sense, along with the pros and cons of each and when to use them.

Don't get bogged down in one versus another. There may be points in time, and depending on the deals, where you would potentially be using several of these simultaneously if you have multiple deals that you are working. So here they are:

TOP 5 FUNDING OPTIONS FOR REAL ESATE INVESTING

1 PAYING CASH
2 PRIVATE MONEY LENDERS
3 HARD MONEY LENDERS
4 SMALL BANK LINES OF CREDIT
5 LONG-TERM MORTGAGE FINANCING

Paying Cash

This source mostly speaks for itself; however, it is worth explaining. Paying cash means exactly that. You are using your money to close a deal.

If you are really new to real estate, this means you will most likely send the funds needed to close via a wire transfer from your bank to the title company's bank. Some title companies may allow a cashier's check, but most don't anymore because there has been too much fraud with them. Personal checks are not allowed (for anything over $1,500), but you have to check with the title company and see what the rules are.

When should you pay cash?

This is a valid question with a surprising answer that's certainly worth discussing. It depends on the deal. If you are in a competitive situation, I believe cash trumps everything else. This means if you have to close this with cash and quickly so you don't lose the deal, then by all means go cash.

Otherwise, it is based on the investing strategy you are choosing. Let's take a look at each one.

REASONS TO PAY CASH
- YOU DON'T WAIT ON ANYONE ELSE FOR THE MONEY
- YOU CAN GENERALLY CLOSE FASTER THAN WITH ANY OTHER SOURCE OF FUNDING
- THERE ARE NO HARD COSTS FOR THE MONEY

REASONS NOT TO PAY CASH
- YOU POTENTIALLY TIE UP A SIGNIFICANT AMOUNT OF MONEY THAT YOU CANNOT USE ELSEWHERE
- IF YOU RUN OUT OF MONEY BECAUSE YOU INCORRECTLY BUDGETED FOR THE IMPROVEMENTS, YOU WILL HAVE TO FIND ANOTHER SOURCE FOR THE FUNDS WHICH CAN CREATE UNANTICIPATED FINANCIAL REPRECUSSIONS
- IF ANOTHER DEAL COMES ALONG, YOU MIGHT END UP HAVING TO PASS ON IT (OPPORTUNITY COST) BECAUSE YOUR MONEY WAS TIED UP IN THIS DEAL

- **Wholesale Deals:** If you are under contract on a deal that you intend to wholesale, and believe you must double close, it would be best to pay cash. This is only if you cannot assign the contract and have to purchase it so you can control the deal until you can sell it.

- **Flipping Property:** If you are flipping the property and personally have the funds necessary to acquire it AND complete all of the tangible improvements (including any unknowns) and will not be strapped for cash that you need in order to live, then by all means pay cash for this and get it done.

- **Rental Property:** When buying a rental property, you almost always want to use financing and not cash for two reasons, unless you absolutely think you will lose the deal.

  1. Despite hearing radio talk show hosts constantly preach about having no debt, it's not a good strategy to grow your real estate business. In fact, using leverage is the most effective way to build a rental portfolio and how almost every successful

real estate investor does it. I agree that having a lot of consumer debt (i.e., personal credit cards, car payments, etc.) is a bad thing. However, debt on real estate used for business purposes that is backed by a tangible asset that produces income does not fall into this category. So, just because you have enough money to pay cash for a rent house, doesn't mean you should ever own it with no debt in place. Remember, the tenant is paying your mortgage, and you will be able to use your cash reserves to buy your next deal.

2. For most conforming loans (as of this writing), you would have to get a cash-out refinance versus a rate-and-term refinance. Under a cash-out refinance, you have to season title and wait 180 days before you can start the financing process. This means you probably won't close on your loan for at least another 30 days, since this is about the average amount of time it takes to complete a conforming loan. In total, you are looking at around 210 days to get your money back.

What if you personally don't have the cash? That's totally okay, and many investors don't. You can move on to numbers 2 through 5 on the list and see which one best suits your needs.

Private Money Lenders

What is a private money lender? Anyone who has money they can loan to you for real estate purchases is someone I would consider a private money lender. Not to get into semantics, but hard money lenders are sometimes called private money lenders.

However, for purposes of our discussion, a private money lender is most likely an individual (not an institution or company). They may loan up to any negotiated LTV, with any negotiated rate and terms, etc. Private money lenders can be family, friends, or someone just wanting to invest in a note secured by real estate.

I consider private money more personal than institutional. They are typically (but not always) less expensive than a hard money lender, but more expensive than a bank or financial institution. Finding a private money lender can take some time. Unless you have family, friends, or someone else you know who is willing to loan you the money for your deal, you will need to find one through your local real estate investing clubs or meetups.

The advantages of using a private lender are many. You can negotiate an interest rate that is probably lower than hard money but higher than a bank. You can also negotiate terms that are very favorable as well (i.e., longer duration, higher LTV, etc.) Why? Many of these lenders operate independently and most likely out of their home (i.e., no staff, no office expense, etc.) They are using their own personal funds so they can do what they want to do. They also may not have as many requirements as a formal hard money lender or financial institution does (i.e., completing an application, submitting your financial information, etc.) You can close relatively quickly with them because they may do the evaluation of the deal themselves.

Some words of caution when using a private money lender. If your lender has never done a loan for real estate investment purposes and doesn't necessarily lend money even on a passive basis, be careful depending on them to close your deal. Many times I have seen where someone was going with a private lender and at the last minute they disappeared on them, wouldn't return their calls, or just decided not to fund the deal for whatever reason. I have even seen the lender create ridiculous terms, causing a situation that is never going to work. This is especially true for someone who has never done this before like a family member or friend.

Why does this happen? One main reason is they may not understand real estate investing. The lender gets nervous and starts to question all of the "what if" scenarios like, "What if you don't pay?" or "What if the property doesn't sell?" or "How do we put the correct paperwork together?"

If this is the case, they probably will not get an appraisal done, and that's a big red flag in my opinion. It's natural for these things to happen, however, it's no fun for the investor who needs to get the deal done.

Hard Money Lenders

I have a lot of experience in this area because I've been in the hard money lending business for years.

Hard money lenders are private (and mostly non-institutional) lenders who loan money to real estate investors, at a defined loan-to-value (LTV) that ranges on average from 65% - 75% of the ARV, typically at higher interest rates (average 12% to 14%) than at a bank or financial institution and on a short term basis (anywhere from six months to one year). This varies of course by lender, but the majority of hard money lenders will loan six months to one year without any extension fees. They typically charge points as well as other fees as part of the loan. The loan amount is based on the ARV and not the purchase price, and can cover some or even all of your rehab and closing costs.

Who uses hard money?

This is a great question and one that confuses almost everyone that is not in the real estate business. When someone asks me what my company does, and I explain it to them, most immediately say, "Oh, so that's for people who can't qualify at a bank and get a loan." Of course I have to explain that this is absolutely not the case and that most of our clients are "A" borrowers (meaning they have excellent financials, low DTI, and excellent credit) and can definitely get a loan at a bank. We have investor clients who have a net worth in the millions, clients who own over 100 properties, and some clients who have used us for almost ten years. We also have new clients who are buying their first property to flip or rent. The bottom line is all types of investors use hard money.

Why do they use hard money if they can go to a bank and get a cheaper rate?

Real estate investors use hard money for many reasons. The primary reason is for convenience. Hard money lenders can close your loan in just a few days. No bank can do this because they require too many things to complete the financing. Banks, which we will discuss next, have guidelines that they have to follow, and are heavily regulated. Depending on the size of your line of credit, it can take a week or two just to get approved because it may have to go before a loan committee that meets once a week or so.

There are just too many delays with banks, and real estate deals (especially good ones) need to close quickly. A hard money borrower can be approved in as little as 30 minutes after they submit their application (which can be a much shorter application than with a bank).

Second to convenience is leverage. You can borrow much more with a hard money loan vs. a bank loan (or line of credit). Since banks have to loan off the cost of the property and not the ARV on a purchase, the loan-to-value is significantly lower and will require the borrower to bring a lot more money to closing than by using hard money. Some banks are also going to require a borrower to have some experience with real estate before they are willing to give you a line of credit where a hard money lender will be more willing to accommodate you.

Using hard money puts another set of eyes on the deal itself, and can provide expertise that a bank is just not going to give you. Nothing against banks and bankers, but they do all types of loans and are not specialists in any one area (for the most part). This means a company like mine that is comprised of real estate investors with years of experience, brings so much more value than a banker just looking at the numbers alone. We can look at a deal and tell our clients right away what the returns are going to be to a very accurate level.

What to look for when choosing a hard money lender

Since I have been in the hard money business, I have had to educate our clients on the value of what a hard money lender brings. When someone calls and is "shopping rates," I cringe because this potential client has no idea what they really need.

The first thing I would look for in a hard money lender is if the people running it have real estate investor experience. So are you talking to a money shop or are you talking to people who know the investor business inside and out? If they are just a money shop, I would move on to the next lender. A lender with no investor experience can lead to a disaster, since they may not have run into the issues you are going to run into when you start working on that house you just bought. When something happens (and it will) and you need to get an answer, having a lender you can rely on is priceless. You can be certain that your banker isn't going to have the answer. Even if they did, you probably don't want to bring that to their attention as it will certainly spook them! There is tremendous value in using a hard money lender and just like with anything else in life, you get what you pay for.

I was not trying to imply earlier that looking for a better interest rate is not important. There are just more important things than rates, and that is usually a catch with lenders I have seen. They offer some super low rate, but when you add up the fees and hidden costs (such as the way they structure the loan), they are far more expensive than the lender with the higher rate.

I would look for someone who is honest about their fees and will explain everything to you up front so there are no surprises. You do need to use caution here and understand any pitfalls in the loan if you go past your term, are late on a payment, or fail to perform. Honest companies will provide you with everything up front so there is no confusion. Talk to other investors and look at the reviews of clients if there are any online before you select your lender.

A Typical Hard Money Loan

A typical hard money loan can look like the following on a house with an ARV of $100,000:

- A loan amount of $70,000 (or 70% of the ARV)
- 3% Origination Points (equates to 3% of the loan amount, or $2,100)
- An administrative, processing, or underwriting fee (can go from $400 - $1,000 depending on what else is being charged)

- $200 - $400 for legal fees (document preparation)
- $400 - $600 for an appraisal
- $75 - $150 for inspection fees for draws

You may be thinking wow that is expensive. Yes, they can be expensive, but are a very valuable tool if used appropriately and with the right lender. Hard money loans can make you very successful as a real estate investor. They are similar to a cash transaction, and most hard money lenders can close very quickly.

Small Bank Line of Credit

The reason I used the term small bank is that a local bank that likes real estate investment loans is going to be your best source for what is called a guidance line of credit for real estate investing. Going to a large commercial bank like Chase Bank, Bank of America, Citibank, etc., is a waste of time because they are not going to give you a line of credit to invest in real estate. You will get frustrated and be very disappointed. Focus on the small community bank in your area. You may have to call around until you find one that is willing to help you. Ask members in online real estate investor forums who they use. You can also ask investors at your local real estate investor club meetings, or in your mastermind group. Someone will be able to direct you to the right one.

No matter which one you find, they are all going to loan based on cost and not the value for purchases, even though they will do an appraisal. This means if you have a house deal that has an ARV of $100,000, a rehab estimate of $20,000 and a purchase price of $50,000, the bank is going to loan around 75% of the appraised value in its current condition or around 80% of cost, whichever is less.

Think about that for a minute. If you are buying any deal, you absolutely want the cost to be less than the value, right? In this scenario you have an excellent deal, but that doesn't matter to the bank. All they care about is the formula I mentioned. So that means you would get a loan amount of $56,000 with an out of pocket amount of $14,000 + closing costs. A hard money lender, on the other hand, is more than likely going to loan you $70,000, putting your out of pocket amount to just your closing costs.

To obtain a small bank line of credit, your banker will more than likely require you to have some experience as a real estate investor. On average, I have seen this be a two-year minimum with investors. You can prove you have this experience with information on your tax returns.

Even though they are heavily regulated, every bank is slightly different when it comes to their specific lending criteria. If you have a significant amount of capital that you can deposit into an account at the bank, you will probably get better treatment if you are lacking in experience. Otherwise, get some experience and then look at using a small bank as another financing resource.

When would you use a small bank line of credit?

You can use this type of financing for any of the investing strategies discussed on acquisitions. However, keep in mind that using one on every purchase you make will require approval from your banker or their loan committee in addition to following all of the other necessary steps to get the transaction closed. This process can take some time and varies by bank. If you have some time to close the transaction (like 30 days), this type of financing may make sense.

The big benefit to this type of financing is much lower interest and fees than hard money. The downside is bankers are typically not real estate investors and the approval process for a deal can be mixed (i.e., if they don't like something about the property, it's not going to get approved). Small banks can also be a great resource for long-term financing, which we will discuss next.

Long-Term Mortgage Financing

When we discuss long-term mortgage financing, we are referring to rental properties only. You would not seek long-term financing to wholesale or flip for obvious reasons. By long-term mortgage financing, I mean 15-year and 30-year loans.

Who offers this type of financing for single-family investment property? Small banks (mostly a 15-year term), GSE's (Government Sponsored Enterprises) like Fannie Mae and Freddie Mac (offering up to 30-year term), and hedge funds (terms vary, but I have seen up to 30-years with balloon payments in ten years). Of course, you can get private money as well and create your own terms.

All of this can be confusing if you are new to the business, so let's dive a bit deeper to understand long-term financing a bit more.

Conventional versus Conforming Mortgage Loans

There are lots of terms thrown around in the industry regarding long-term mortgage financing. Let's clear them up a bit so there is no confusion.

The term *conventional mortgage* means any mortgage loan that is not insured or backed by the federal government. Small bank loans are conventional loans.

A *conforming mortgage* loan is one that abides by (or conforms to) the guidelines set by Fannie Mae or Freddie Mac. These guidelines include loan-to-value ratio (LTV), the borrower's credit score, along with the borrower's DTI.

This means that if you want one of these loans, you will have to conform to their minimum requirements for each of these guidelines. They offer 30-year amortizations, with the lowest market rate of interest, and the fees a lender can charge you are somewhat regulated. A Fannie Mae or Freddie Mac loan on a rental property is going to give you the best cash flow due to this lower rate and longer term. There is also a limit to the number of loans Fannie/Freddie will give you, and as of this writing, you are allowed to have ten financed properties with them.

Why not start with a long-term mortgage loan first?

Wouldn't it save time, money, and effort to do one loan instead of two? Great questions. The answer is you cannot get a conforming loan on a house that requires anything more than basic touchup paint and carpet cleaning.

If any mechanical equipment is missing (i.e., hot water heater, condensing unit, air handler, etc.) or is just disconnected, the house will not be approved for financing until these items are addressed. If the roof is visibly worn beyond its functional use and there are leaks present, it will probably be noted in the appraisal report that a satisfactory roof inspection is required. The same holds true for the foundation if there is evidence of settlement where there are cracks in the walls. This will certainly be noted and/or photographed in the appraisal.

Appraisers are not inspectors, but they can recommend an engineer's report, or suggest that repairs are needed in their appraisal. So if the seller is willing to give you the time to close with a conforming loan and the house needs very little in terms of repairs, by all means go straight to into a long-term mortgage.

Small Bank Mortgage Financing

In my opinion, the best time to use small bank mortgage financing is after you have exhausted your loan limit with Fannie Mae or Freddie Mac. The good news here is you will have gained some experience on your first few (or ten) deals, and will probably be buying deals even better by the time you get to using a small bank.

As I stated, small banks are most likely going to offer 15-year terms (some will go to 20 years) with or without a balloon payment, and will have a fixed rate of interest for the first so many years (i.e., three years fixed, five years fixed, etc.) This means that the rate can increase or decrease after a specific date.

Be sure to run your numbers to make sure you can cash flow with the initial rate as well as any potential rate increase. Some small banks will allow you to finance the purchase, provide funds to complete any necessary rehab/repairs, and convert to an amortized loan over a longer term. But remember, the loan amount will be based on the cost of the property.

Hedge Fund Financing

Hedge funds operate on their own set of terms, which can vary greatly depending on which one you are using. As of this writing, there are several national hedge funds that will loan on rental property and generally like to finance larger portfolios of rentals and/or have a minimum loan amount, like $500,000, in order to originate a loan. Most of the loans are packaged and put into some type of bond fund.

Be sure to do your due diligence and read the fine print before you sign up for one of these loans. Although the qualification process, rate, and term can be attractive, there can be pre-payment fees if you pay the loan off early, balloon payments (a payoff after so many years in the loan), as well as mandatory maintenance and repairs that must be escrowed with your monthly payment.

CHAPTER 21

IS IT A GOOD TIME TO INVEST IN REAL ESTATE?

Now that we have a better understanding of real estate investing, we need to take a closer look at how timing can impact it. Why? Because one of the most common questions I hear from new investors is, "Is it a good time to be in real estate?" The answer to this question is YES! However, because this is such a loaded question, it really needs some further explanation. I have two things I want you to keep in mind about this:

1. First, *no one has a crystal ball* where they can accurately predict the future. With that said, it is important to understand where you are in your market cycle so you can adjust your investing strategy accordingly.

2. Second, *nothing will prevent you from getting started with your real estate investing career more than worrying about things you cannot control.* Once you determine specifically what you are going to do in real estate investing, you can adapt to your current market and take the most effective approach to maximizing your returns.

THE REAL ESTATE MARKET IS CYCLICAL

Real estate, just like any other market, goes in cycles. There is a lot of information out there about this subject. Without diving into all of the economic indicators that impact real estate (as well as other industries), let's take a look at it from a high level.

Glenn Mueller, PhD and real estate market cycle expert, says that real estate cycles go through four different phases:

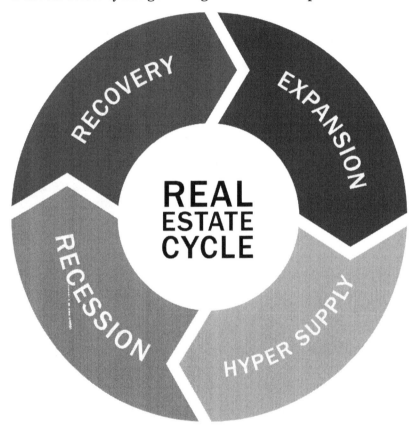

If you want to learn more about this, read his article that he wrote in 2001 titled, "Predicting Long-Term Trends & Market Cycles In Commercial Real Estate."

How long do these real estate cycles last? Some believe the real estate market moves in 7-10 year cycles. Fred Foldvary, who is a highly credible economist and predicted the 2008 real estate market crash in 1997, believes the market moves in 18-year cycles.

So which is it, the seven- to ten-year cycle, the eighteen-year cycle, or some other cycle? No one really knows for sure, but there are ways you can see what phase your market is in based on how it is behaving. We will address this at the end of the chapter. For now, understand that every market is different as are its trends.

The real estate market cycle can go on for a longer or shorter period of time than what may be expected. Also, there is no way to accurately predict what is going to happen in the market, and you certainly don't want to overanalyze it to the point that you are too afraid to get started investing in real estate.

WHAT AFFECTS THE REAL ESTATE MARKET'S CYCLE?

While there are many factors that can impact the real estate market on a national level, you will want to focus on those that are impacting your local market. Take these into account before implementing your investing strategy to determine whether or not they are going to affect you. Let's go over what I believe are the top three factors that CAN affect the value of real estate in your market at any given time:

1. Specific economic conditions in your local real estate market like the availability of housing and the corresponding demand (basic supply and demand), are the most important considerations. Your local economy (i.e., jobs and other economic activity) has the biggest impact on the real estate cycle in your market.

2. The forces behind mortgage financing (like we saw before the 2008 crash) can also play a tremendous role on a macro scale that impacts every market in the country. Most mortgage financing is provided by federally backed loans from Fannie Mae, Freddie

Mac, FHA (Federal Housing Administration), or VA (Veterans Administration). These lenders have specific guidelines that change over time and impact a borrower's qualifications. The stricter the guidelines, the fewer the eligible borrowers.

3. Mortgage interest rates play a major role in the real estate market cycle and change, sometimes multiple times, each day. It's important to understand that mortgage interest rates should not be confused with the Fed raising interest rates. These two rates are completely different from one another. For all intents and purposes, mortgage interest rates are determined by the bond market, and not necessarily what the Fed is doing or going to do. As mortgage rates increase (while housing prices remain flat or increase), mortgage payments will also increase, making it more difficult for someone to qualify for the same priced house as when rates were lower.

There are other national factors and major economic indicators that can have an effect on the market but may not necessarily be impacting your local market. However, you may turn on the news and think differently. Many people not in the real estate business focus too much on this, which can lead to never doing anything at all.

AVOID BAD INFORMATION ABOUT YOUR MARKET

Don't let your local news media (i.e., TV, newspaper, or radio) influence your real estate investing. These outlets are in the business of selling advertising and can inflate or exaggerate what's really happening in your world. Some of it can be sensationalized to the point of scaring those both in and out of the business. For example, in Dallas, TX a local newspaper real estate writer recently wrote an article (Fall of 2015) about how real estate prices in the major markets in Texas have reached an "unsustainable" level and are "overvalued." Whenever you see or hear words like "unsustainable" or "overvalued," exercise some caution.

In the same article, there was a chart that illustrated this by the percentage believed to be unsustainable based on historical pricing before the previous recession. While there may be some truth to some of the numbers in some of the markets, history doesn't repeat itself the same way every time. Market forces dictate if a market is overvalued, not historical analysis.

The article went on to say that prices in North Texas are now 20% higher than before the recession. The recession started in 2008 after the financial crisis. This article was written in 2015. In a normal, healthy market like we have in North Texas, real estate values increase about 2-3% per year (also known as market appreciation). So if we are up 20% since the recession started (when values were depressed), that's an average of 2-3% per year, over the course of 7 years, and the market is catching up to where it would have been normally. Every market is different so verify the trends where you are investing.

Keep in mind, your timing in the market really depends on what you are trying to accomplish. Flipping property can be very time sensitive depending on where you are in the market cycle. For example, if you are trying to flip houses in a downward trending market (which you can absolutely have success doing), you may be subject to pricing pressure, and may need to adjust your purchase price to a lower amount.

The same thing holds true for rental properties. Recessions can put downward pressure on rental rates, whereas high periods of inflation can put upward pressure on rents (meaning you can raise rental rates). However, you can make money in any market if you buy the deal correctly.

The point here is to understand what type of market you are in and adjust your investing program accordingly. Don't let the market keep you from investing in real estate; you can be profitable in almost any market.

Also, when you hear the national news media talk about real estate prices going up or down, you may want to use some caution and focus on your local market for information. This macro level information may not have an impact on what you are doing because your local market may be completely different from what is going on everywhere else.

UTILIZING EXPERTS IN YOUR MARKET

So how can you determine what is actually going on in your market/sub-market? Real estate agents who are actively working that specific market (meaning someone who is full time in the business and does not just hold a license) typically know what is going on at the present time better than anyone. The residents that live there will probably know what houses are selling for and may know some market data because they live in the area. Appraisers, who can cover areas much larger than most real estate agents, have a broader sense of the market as a whole and can analyze the market on a macro scale. If you talk to all three, there is no doubt you will know exactly what is going on in this particular market.

Appraisers, as part of their business practice, rely on real estate agents/brokers to explain nuances at the sub-market level when working on an appraisal. I have found over time that some appraisers study the broader market and analyze trends and patterns, while others do not. The appraisers who do this type of research are great to call on to see what the trend is in the overall market. Build a relationship with one (or more) of them and get their thoughts on what the market is doing.

By the way, any appraiser has access to the information, but not every one of them is going to be a reliable resource for this information. However, I rely on both real estate agents and appraisers depending on the type of information I am trying to get. Once you start your real estate business and transact some deals, you are going to get a feel for the market. Your mastermind group will eventually help with seeing local trends because you can get a perspective from a broader range of people actively in the business.

KEY MARKET INDICATORS

To further understand what is going on in your target market, focus your attention on the following three key market indicators to understand the trend: (1) Median Sales Price, (2) Months of Supply, and (3) Days on Market (DOM). Let's cover them here and discuss how to go about getting this information.

Median Sales Price

By definition, this is the middle list price (not the average) of the houses listed on the market. For example, if you have houses listed at $100,000, $150,000, $200,000, $250,000 and $600,000, the median price would be $200,000. The average would be $260,000. The reason median is used instead of average is it more accurately represents the set of data being evaluated where averages do not. If the $600,000 house were $1,000,000, that would give an average list price of $340,000, which is not an accurate reflection of this market as you have a $1,000,000 home skewing the numbers. Therefore, the median sales price is used in conjunction with Months of Supply and DOM to analyze a market and determine its trend.

A great way to do this is to track the Median Sales Price over the past 12 months (from your current month) and analyze the trend in terms of a percentage. Is it headed up (could be a positive market trend) or down (possibly a negative trend) or is it flat (maybe it's a stable market), and by what percentage?

Months of Supply

By definition this means how many months it would take for all of the available properties on the market for sale to actually sell. For example, if you look at the MLS for a given area and see that there are currently 90 homes on the market with 30 homes selling each month, that would indicate that there is a three-month supply left in the market (90 / 30 = 3). If this is what is going on in your market, then that would indicate that your market is strong. If you are in a market like this, selling a property is much easier.

Conversely, if you have 90 homes on the market and only 9 selling each month, that would indicate a 10-month supply and not a very strong market. The weaker the market, the more downward pressure there is on pricing.

If you have 24 homes on the market and one sold, that means there is a two-year supply of homes. This could indicate a very slow and weak market, and you need to be very careful if you are flipping in a market like this. You may need to try to whole-sale or buy rentals instead of flip houses. In my opinion, if there were a two-year supply of houses on the market in a given area, I would not try to flip a house there. Your potential to get stuck holding this for the duration is really high.

So where is the cutoff point for flipping a house in terms of supply? A six-month supply is considered normal or stable. Anything over a six-month supply is probably something that would require further market evaluation. You need to ask questions like why is the months of supply greater than six months? What are the factors that are influencing this higher supply, and when is it anticipated that they will be corrected? This is an area that can create an over analysis, but I want to point it out so you are aware of it. It will probably not be hard to determine, and if you have lived in the area for a while, you probably already know the answer. Look at all of the data and get some feedback from experts before deciding to invest here or not at this time.

Days on Market

By definition Days on Market (also abbreviated as DOM) is the length of time a real estate listing is on the market for sale, and it is the next key indicator that you need to consider. This is a different number than Months of Supply since it applies to an individual property.

I like to look at all of the listings for sale and see what the average Days on Market is for that specific area as well and if there are any anomalies (ones that are too high for some reason). I would strip those out and focus on the rest of the ones in the list you are analyzing.

In my opinion, if the average DOM is >180, that's a sign that the market is slow. That means it's taking, on average, six months to sell a house. Anything past six months is of concern. If it's just a couple of houses that are on the market, and they are distressed, they may still be overpriced, and I would probably not worry too much about it. If, however, they are in very good condition, had enough market exposure, and are just not selling, they are probably overpriced.

Getting and Using This Information

So how do you get the Median Sales Price, Months of Supply, and Days on Market (DOM)? Do you need to do this yourself? Of course you don't. You can rely on your agent, broker, or appraiser to give you this information. However, if you have access to the MLS, there is probably some type of reporting available for you to analyze these numbers, which is where this information originates.

If I were flipping a house and the Months of Supply is approaching 12 with the average DOM >180, I would be cautious and consult with your agent or broker (who knows this area) to get their thoughts on the state of the market and go from there. I would also bounce this off your appraiser to get their insight. However, if the Median Sales Price showed an increase in 10% (over the past 12 months), Months of Supply were two, and DOM was 30, that would indicate a very strong market where you should feel comfortable wholesaling or flipping. Keep in mind these indicators do not apply to the rental market.

Most new investors never look at any of these indicators, which is a big mistake. Knowing what they are in your market will give you the confidence you need to be a successful real estate investor.

<u>Appendix</u>

Glossary

The following is a compilation of all glossary sections. This list is organized alphabetically instead of by section to make it easier to use as a reference.

Appraisal: This is a report performed by a licensed real estate appraiser that provides the value of a property based on market facts, as well as subjectivity, along with how that value was determined.

AS IS: The property is in its current condition, no matter what that condition is.

Close (or Closing): refers to when a real estate transaction between a buyer and seller is finalized. The documents related to the conveying of title are executed by all parties. This usually takes place at a title company. Once everything is executed and approved (if an approval is required by a lender) the transaction can be funded. Funding occurs when money changes hands.

Draws: A monetary amount used to fund any work being done to a property. For example, you have a loan on a property with the repair portion being held by your lender until the work is complete. Once you complete some (or all) of the work (depending on your agreement with your lender) you can request that the funds be reimbursed to you. This is done in the form of a draw request.

Earnest Money: A monetary deposit made payable to a seller (usually at the title company facilitating the transaction) that shows the buyer's good faith in the contract that was executed between them. Example – Joe put down $2,000 earnest money in his contract with Tom and sent it to American Title for them to hold.

Equity: The difference between the ARV and total acquisition cost of the property, which may or may not include your closing costs, depending on how you wish to calculate it.

Foreclosure Listings: In Texas, properties on a foreclosure list are those that are posted at the courthouse steps 21 days prior to the auction where they are scheduled for foreclosure.

Functional Obsolescence: According to the *Dictionary of Real Estate Appraisal, Fifth Edition* (Appraisal Institute), functional obsolescence is "the impairment of functional capacity of a property according to market tastes and standards." The Appraisal Institute's book, *The Appraisal of Real Estate, Thirteenth Edition,* states, "Functional obsolescence may be caused by a deficiency or a superadequacy. Some forms are curable and others are incurable."

—**Deficiency**: a type of functional obsolescence that is basically the lack of something that other properties in the subject's neighborhood have. An example would be a poor floor plan that has a bedroom that can only be accessed through another bedroom.

—**Superadequacy**: a type of functional obsolescence that exceeds what is typical for the properties in the area and does not contribute to the overall value in an amount equal to its cost (i.e., putting $30,000 worth of appliances in a house worth $90,000).

FSBO (For Sale By Owner): When a seller sells a property, without the assistance of a broker.

Garage Conversion: This involves transforming a functional garage (one that is typically and primarily used for automobile storage as well as storage for tools/equipment/supplies and other items not stored inside the premises) into livable space.

HUD: An acronym for the Department of Housing and Urban Development.

Market Appreciation: When the value of a property increases due to positive changes in the market.

Memorandum of Contract: A document that gets recorded in the county of record that states that a buyer has a contract with a seller for a specific property address that was executed on a specific date. This document becomes a public record allowing title companies to find it and prevent a closing on a property that is under contract with another party. For example, Bob (the buyer) gets a property under contract with Susan (the seller) and records his interest in their contract with a memorandum of contract. Bob is the executor of the memorandum, believes he has a great deal that he negotiated, and does not want Susan to go around him and get someone else under contract.

MLS (Multiple Listing Service): By definition, a private offer of cooperation and compensation by listing brokers to other real estate brokers. The MLS is a tool to help listing brokers find co-operative brokers working with buyers to help sell their clients' homes. MLSs are private databases that are created, maintained, and paid for by real estate professionals to help their clients buy and sell property. Realtor.org is the source of this definition. The majority of properties for sale in a given market are more than likely listed by licensed brokers on their respective MLS. Sellers of property are under a listing agreement with the broker allowing them to disseminate information about the property that other brokers and users of the system can access. Listings on the MLS typically include (but are not limited to) the property address, a description of the property, number of bedrooms, baths, square footage, year built, school district, days on market, listing broker contact information, etc.

Mortgage Calculator: A calculator that determines what your mortgage payment will be based on the following variables – interest rate, term (length of the actual mortgage) and principal amount of the mortgage.

Option Fee: This has multiple definitions, but for purposes of this book it means a monetary amount made payable to a seller from a buyer, for consideration to have the opportunity to terminate a contract between them for any reason, within a specified period of time. For example, Paul (the buyer) gave John (the seller) a $200 option check for ten days to decide if he wants to move forward with the transaction. This is also referred to as the option period or inspection period as this is when properties are inspected.

Pocket Buyer: A reliable investor that can be called directly to purchase a property from a seller (typically a wholesaler).

Probate: The legal process for proving that a will is valid through a court of law that occurs after a person has died. The court publishes a list that displays the assets of the deceased in what is known as a probate listing.

Real Estate Agent: Someone who acts as an intermediary between buyers and sellers in transactions of real property. Agents have a fiduciary responsibility to their clients. They are sometimes referred to as real estate brokers, but it depends on the state in which they are operating. According to Realtor.com, anyone who earns a real estate license can be called a real estate agent. State requirements vary, but in all states you must take a minimum number of classes and pass a test to earn your license.

Real Estate Appraiser: A professionally licensed expert who assesses a property to estimate or determine the value via a documented report called an appraisal.

Real Estate Broker: Someone who acts as an intermediary between buyers and sellers in transactions of real property, who has taken the additional education requirements beyond those required to become an agent, and passed a broker exam. Brokers can act as an agent and the term "broker" is sometimes used interchangeably with the term agent, depending on where they are located. Brokers can have agents (or other brokers) working under their license.

Realtor: By definition, a real estate agent who is a member of the National Association of REALTORS®, which means that he or she must uphold the standards of the association and its code of ethics. The term Realtor is trademarked.

REOs (Real Estate Owned by the bank): The technical term for describing a bank foreclosed property.

Seller Concessions: Contributions made to a buyer at the time of closing to pay for closing costs and costs related to the buyer's financing. It is basically a gift from the seller to the buyer, which effectively lowers the purchase price of the property.

Sold Comparable (Sold Comp): This refers to a property that most closely resembles the property you are evaluating for purchase.

Subject Property: This refers to the specific deal that you are evaluating for purchase.

Title Company: A neutral, third party that assists in the conveyance (the transfer) of ownership between sellers and buyers of real property. Title companies make sure that the title (ownership) to a given property is legitimate and offer insurance on the title (through a title policy) to the buyer and also to a lender (through what is called a mortgagee's title policy) if the property is going to be financed.

Total Acquisition Cost: The formula for this is:
Purchase Price + Rehab Amount (Scope of Work) + Closing Costs = Total Acquisition Cost

2.A EXAMPLE MAIL CAMPAIGN LETTER

I WANT TO BUY YOUR !
PROPERTY FOR CASH !

Month DD, YYYY

Owner Name
Owner Address
Owner City, ST ZIP

Dear First Name,

I am currently buying homes in Subject City, and would like to make you an **ALL CASH OFFER** for your property at Subject Address. **IF YOU ARE INTERESTED IN SELLING, HERE IS WHY YOU SHOULD SELL TO ME:**

• I buy in **"as-is" condition** so you don't do any repairs
• You will not have to hire an agent or broker
• I will **pay for all of your closing costs**
• We can **close in about a week**, or as soon as you are ready

Please call me at Phone Number to discuss selling your property. If you reach my voice mail, please leave a message and I will call you back as soon as possible. Thank you for your time.

Sincerely,

Your Name
Acquisitions Manager

P.S. - Not interested in selling now? Keep this with your important real estate papers.

2.B EXAMPLE MAIL CAMPAIGN POSTCARD

2.C SOW SPREADSHEET

SCOPE OF WORK TEMPLATE

PROPERTY ADDRESS:
REPAIR AMOUNT:

SCOPE OF WORK LINE ITEMS	DESCRIPTION OF LINE ITEM	LOCATION OF LINE ITEM
DEMOLITION WORK		
FOUNDATION		
FRAMING		
ROOFING		
WINDOWS		
EXTERIOR DOORS		
ELECTRICAL		
PLUMBING FIXTURES		
DUCTWORK FOR HVAC		
HVAC - AIR HANDLER		
HVAC - CONDENSING UNIT		
INSULATION		
SHEETROCK		
TAPED-BED-TEXTURE		
INTERIOR PAINT		
EXTERIOR PAINT		
BRICK / SIDING		
FIREPLACE		
INTERIOR TRIM / DOORS		
CABINETRY		
COUNTER TOPS		
TILE - BATH & ENTRY		
ELECTRICAL FIXTURES		
HARDWARE		
APPLIANCES		
FLOORING - TILE		
FLOORING - CARPET/WOOD/LAMINATE		
FLATWORK / DRIVES		
FENCE		
DUMPSTER		
CLEAN-UP		
LANDSCAPE		
TOTAL		

SCOPE OF WORK	% OF SOW	% COMPLETED	$ COMPLETED	REMAINING
$		0%	$	$
$		0%	$	$
$		0%	$	$
$		0%	$	$
$		0%	$	$
$		0%	$	$
$		0%	$	$
$		0%	$	$
$		0%	$	$
$		0%	$	$
$		0%	$	$
$		0%	$	$
$		0%	$	$
$		0%	$	$
$		0%	$	$
$		0%	$	$
$		0%	$	$
$		0%	$	$
$		0%	$	$
$		0%	$	$
$		0%	$	$
$		0%	$	$
$		0%	$	$
$		0%	$	$
$		0%	$	$
$		0%	$	$
$		0%	$	$
$		0%	$	$
$		0%	$	$
$		0%	$	$
$		0%	$	$
$		0%	$	$
$		0%	$	$

Acknowledgements

There are many people to thank for their assistance with this book. First, I want to thank my family that I love very much and thank God for every day. As you go through life, you have moments when you reflect on why you do what you do. This is especially true during challenging times, when your family is all you need to see to keep yourself motivated. I love what I do and wouldn't want to do anything else, and I do it because I love them very much and always want the best for them.

A big thank you goes to Rich Allen, my business coach and consultant, who has advised me over the past several years and helped me take my lending business to the next level. It was his idea that I share my knowledge by writing this book. Without him, I would have never done it.

Throughout the process of completing this text, I relied on Tracy Card and Jennifer Webb who provided feedback regarding the copy, as well as editing of the text. In addition to being so smart and reliable, their background as real estate investors had a thorough impact on the content. I would probably still be in writing mode if it were not for them. Thank you Tracy and Jennifer!

I have to thank all of my clients that I have loaned money to over the years on their real estate deals. Seeing what they have gone through, coupled with my personal experience as an investor, has given me a unique perspective that has brought much more value to this text.

I also want to thank Clark Waggoner who helped me understand what it takes to write a book effectively and have the most impact, in addition to providing the structure, flow, as well as the professional editing. I learned a lot from him and thank him very much.

Shannon Durst has helped me so much over the years with her incredible talent as a visual designer. She designed the cover along with all of the images inside the copy, and also helped with the title by bringing an outsider's viewpoint into perspective. A big thanks goes out to you Shannon.

Finally, I need to thank Jonathan Peters, PhD, who helped with organizing the layout and provided some final editing. As an author and professional writer himself, Jonathan took over the most difficult part, which is taking a finished copy through all of the necessary steps to get a book published. I couldn't have done this without him.